OCT 08 2001

# John Chapman

# Other titles in *Historical American Biographies*

Historical American Biographies

# JOHN CHAPMAN

## The Legendary Johnny Appleseed

Karen Clemens Warrick

**Enslow Publishers, Inc.**

| | |
|---|---|
| 40 Industrial Road | PO Box 38 |
| Box 398 | Aldershot |
| Berkeley Heights, NJ 07922 | Hants GU12 6BP |
| USA | UK |

http://www.enslow.com

**Library of Congress Cataloging-in-Publication Data**

Warrick, Karen Clemens.
John Chapman : the legendary Johnny Appleseed / Karen Clemens Warrick.
    p. cm. — (Historical American biographies)
Includes bibliographical references and index.
ISBN 0-7660-1443-6
1. Appleseed, Johnny, 1774–1845—Juvenile literature. 2. Apple growers—
   United States—Biography—Juvenile literature. 3. Frontier and pioneer
   life—Middle West—Juvenile literature. [1. Appleseed, Johnny, 1774–1845.
   2. Apple growers. 3. Frontier and pioneer life.] I. Title. II. Series.
SB63.A6 W37 2001

634'.11'092—dc21

                              00-009661

Printed in the United States of America

10 9 8 7 6 5 4 3 2

**To Our Readers:** We have done our best to make sure all Internet addresses in
this book were active and appropriate when we went to press. However, the
author and the publisher have no control over and assume no liability for the
material available on those Internet sites or on other Web sites they may link to.
Any comments or suggestions can be sent by e-mail to comments@enslow.com or
to the address on the back cover.

# CONTENTS

# *Acknowledgments*

I wish to thank my uncle, James A. Watson, who helped me locate resources in and around Mansfield, Ohio, and took some of the photographs included in this book.

I also want to thank the Allen County-Fort Wayne Historical Society, librarians at the Leominster and Mansfield public libraries, and a special thanks to the Allen County Public Library in Fort Wayne, which generously granted permission to reprint documents from *The Johnny Appleseed Sourcebook* by Robert C. Harris.

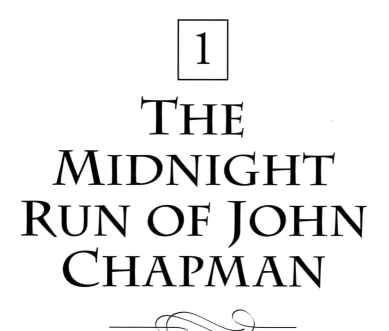

# 1

# THE MIDNIGHT RUN OF JOHN CHAPMAN

On August 21, 1812, just north of Mansfield in what was then the Ohio wilderness (and today is located in the central part of Ohio), John Chapman sounded the alarm, "Flee for your lives—the Canadians and Indians are landing at Huron!"[1] This was reported by Mrs. Hanson Reed and her sons, homesteaders who were building a new home and farm along the Huron River. At the time, the Shawnee, Delaware, and Wyandot Indians still greatly outnumbered the white settlers.

It was late afternoon when Chapman's voice was heard in the clearing where the family's log cabin stood. Hanson Reed was out in the woods, rounding up his cows for milking. The Reeds and two other families, the Palmers and the Smiths, quickly collected some household goods. They hid their most valuable possessions in the woods and started off along the trail that followed the Huron River south toward Mansfield, a settlement of fewer than twelve families. It was getting dark and rain had fallen during the day. The muddy ground made walking difficult. Part of the way, a path had to be cut through the underbrush. It was a terrifying journey for the pioneer families.[2]

The next morning, a special messenger en route from Fort Detroit in the Michigan Territory to Washington, D.C., passed through Mansfield. He brought news of the most recent battle of the War of 1812. The United States' second war with Great Britain was being fought to protect United States neutrality at sea and to ensure American independence. The British now controlled Fort Detroit. General Isaac Brock had defeated the commander of the American forces, Brigadier General William Hull.

The messenger also reported that two thousand Indians under British command were on their way to Sandusky, Ohio. The settlement on the shore of Lake Erie was only about seventy miles north of Mansfield. Based on this report, the homesteaders decided to remain near the blockhouse. It was a log fort built on the town square to provide a safe refuge during an attack.

**False Alarm**

The settlers eventually learned that Chapman's first warning was a false alarm.

Chapman had been hired by the Reeds, Palmers, and Smiths to travel the seventy miles to Lake Erie at least once a week and warn them of danger from the British and American Indians. When he learned that boats loaded with soldiers had landed near the Huron River, he spread the alarm.

The boats actually held American prisoners, soldiers who had been captured after the defeat of Fort Detroit. Under the terms of General Hull's surrender, the prisoners were sent by water to the nearest landing on the south shore of Lake Erie and released.

When no attacks were reported in the area during the next few days, the Mansfield settlers felt safe enough to go out into the woods. Then one September evening, Levi Jones, the local merchant, grocer, and whiskey vendor, was ambushed, killed, and scalped while returning to town along a trail through the woods. Two men working nearby heard the shots and Jones's cries. They raced to Mansfield to sound the alarm.

The settlers soon discovered that Hanson Reed and John Wallace were missing. Fearing that these two men had also been murdered and that Indians

would attack at any moment, the settlers hurried inside the one-room blockhouse. It measured thirty by thirty feet and easily held all the settlers living within a twelve-mile radius of Mansfield.

The families still did not feel safe, however. There were no troops to defend them and everyone felt sure the British and Indians would attack by morning. They decided to send a messenger for help.

*The historic Mansfield blockhouse in which the Reeds, Palmers, Smiths, and other settlers in the surrounding territory took refuge on that fateful September night has been preserved in a Mansfield city park.*

The sun had set. Stars were beginning to shine. The nearest troops were stationed twenty-six miles away at Mount Vernon, Ohio. The trip to find help would have to be made in the dark through the wilderness—a forest full of bears, wolves, and hostile Indians. The settlers wondered who would agree to go on this dangerous journey.

Someone finally stepped forward and said, "I'll go."[3] The thirty-eight-year-old volunteer was John Chapman, better known in the Mansfield area as Johnny Appleseed.

Chapman's journey to Mount Vernon was a mission to warn the countryside of danger. Chapman reportedly ran through the night—barefoot—over a newly cut, rough road. At each cabin scattered along his route, Chapman would rap on the door and warn the settlers of danger with this message, recorded years later:

> The Spirit of the Lord is upon me, and he hath anointed me to blow the trumpet in the wilderness, and sound an alarm in the forest; for behold, the tribes of the heathen are round about your doors, and a devouring flame followeth after them.[4]

After arousing each family with his call, John Chapman advised them to flee to the blockhouse. He did not eat or sleep until he had warned every settler and reached his destination.

In Mount Vernon, Chapman woke the garrison commander, Captain William Douglas, and informed

him of the trouble. Douglas immediately mustered his troops. By three in the morning, they were marching back along the wilderness road.

When Chapman and the troops arrived at the Mansfield blockhouse shortly after daybreak, they found all the settlers, including Wallace and Reed, safe inside. The two had returned soon after Chapman had left for Mount Vernon. They had not been harmed.

Now that the troops had arrived and the immediate threat of attack was over, the settlers laughed at the silly things they had done in their fright. Samuel Wilson's behavior earned him the biggest laugh. He had run all the way to the blockhouse with just his overcoat on, carrying his pantaloons (trousers) under his arm.[5]

The settlers also marveled at John Chapman, who had made the round trip of fifty-two miles between sunset and sunrise to bring help so quickly. When asked how he had accomplished this extraordinary feat, Chapman is said to have replied that God gives strength for the appointed task.

## History or Legend?

John Chapman's marathon run through the wilderness in September 1812 to alert the local people of danger has remained one of the best-known stories of the Ohio frontier. His warning cries that roused settlers from their beds were not forgotten, and his words were repeated as the story was handed down from one generation to another. Chapman's midnight run was celebrated in tales and verse. It finally became legend after W. D. Haley's story "Johnny Appleseed—A Pioneer Hero," was published in *Harper's New Monthly Magazine* in November 1871.

Although Haley's tale seemed to be based on the seeds of truth, those seeds sprouted and grew into a legend larger than the real-life hero. Readers of the time did not question the facts. And since no one bothered to record Chapman's story in 1812, today we are left to wonder which parts are history and which parts are pure legend.

**John Chapman, Friend**
Chapman's historic run during the War of 1812 is remembered in this poem by Helen Woods Richardson:

*A thirty mile trek*
*From dusk to light,*
*To bid the good neighbors—*
*"Beware! Beware!"*

*A shout in the dark—*
*A cry thru' the night—*
*"The red-skins are coming,*
*Prepare! Prepare!"*[6]

[The derogatory term *redskins* was commonly used during Chapman's time.]

*This illustration of Chapman's run through the night from Mansfield to Mount Vernon, was published with W. D. Haley's story "Johnny Appleseed—A Pioneer Hero."*

According to Anthony Banning Norton, the earliest historian in Knox County, Ohio (where Mansfield was then located), and all reliable records and accounts available, Chapman did make his famous trip, but he did not go to Mount Vernon. The regiment stationed there was away on a scouting mission, so Chapman could not have expected to find help there.

It is more likely that Chapman traveled twenty-one miles south to Fredericktown, not on foot, but on horseback. The purpose of his trek was to sound the alarm at each and every homestead scattered about the district. And Chapman was the best candidate for that job. While searching for sites to plant apple seeds, he had wandered all across the woods and hills surrounding Mansfield. It is quite likely that no one else was familiar enough with the territory to have found every isolated cabin and have warned all the homesteaders. While this version of Chapman's midnight ride seems to be historically accurate, storytellers prefer the more romantic tale of Chapman's barefoot run to Mount Vernon.

# 2

# THE
# MINUTEMAN'S
# SON

Excitement was in the air in the fall of 1774 as the First Congregational Church clerk recorded: "John Chapman, Sun [*sic*] of Nathaniael and Elizabeth Chapman, Born at Leominster September ye 26th 1774."[1]

The stir was because the more than nine hundred inhabitants in the Massachusetts Bay Colony village of Leominster were preparing for war. All through the summer, settlers heard drums roll and fifes play. They watched as troops marched back and forth across the green, or meadow, in front of the town meetinghouse. Throughout September 1774, the militia, an army of village men and boys,

drilled daily. Dressed in homemade coats and breeches, they practiced marching with their guns.[2] Crowds from the village and surrounding farms cheered on the ninety-nine volunteers.

A couple of weeks later, the town gathered for General Muster Day, the day selected by the Worcester County Assembly for towns to convene and choose officers to command the militia. The minutemen of Leominster, volunteers who promised to be ready to fight at a minute's notice, paraded. The regiment included more than half the town's 173 boys and men between the ages of sixteen and sixty. No two soldiers were dressed alike. Some carried muskets, others only stout sticks. The patchwork crew performed enthusiastically in the name of the Commonwealth of Massachusetts, demanding the right to govern themselves. Massachusetts Bay

**A Legendary Birth**

Though John Chapman was actually born in the fall, not in the spring when trees bloom, storytellers often tell this tale: On the day Chapman, later known as Johnny Appleseed, was born, apple blossoms on a tree reached down and tapped at the Chapman window. When he opened his tiny eyes, he reached up his hands and cried for the beautifully fragrant blossoms.

Colony citizens no longer wished to be subjects of Great Britain. And they all promised to fight to protect their independence.

Elizabeth Chapman held baby John, not yet a month old, as she stood in the crowd. Her brother, Zebedee Simons, and her husband, Nathaniel, were part of the military parade. Her four-year-old daughter, Elizabeth, stood by her side.

## Family Ties

Elizabeth Simons Chapman was the fifth of nine children. Her ancestors had sailed into Boston on the *Planter* in 1635 and settled in nearby Woburn, Massachusetts, around 1644. James Simons (also spelled Simonds or Symonds), Elizabeth's father, was one of Leominster's first settlers. He had come to the Nashua Valley in May 1740 and built an ordinary frame house that stood for one hundred fifty years.

Nathaniel Chapman's great-great-great-great-grandfather landed in Boston in 1639, and settled in Ipswich, Massachusetts. He died in 1678, and left his wife "thirty good-bearing apple trees."[3] A love of orcharding was part of the Chapman family heritage.

When Nathaniel Chapman was only six years old, his mother died. He rarely spoke about his childhood and always claimed that the most important day of his life was when he married his love, Elizabeth Simons, in August 1769.[4]

*John was born in the fall when apples are picked, so he could not have smelled the fragrant apple blossoms on the day of his birth. These apple blossoms are growing on the last surviving tree that John Chapman planted in the Ohio Territory.*

Nathaniel, a farmer and carpenter, harvested grain and took whatever carpentry jobs he could find to earn a living. He never made enough money to buy his own land, so he rented a few acres from Jonathan Johnson of Woburn, whose wife was a cousin of Elizabeth Simons Chapman. He grew corn, potatoes, and turnips to feed his family. The Chapmans were poor. They could not even afford to buy a cow—"For they are very scarce and dear," Elizabeth wrote in a letter.[5]

## A Revolution Brewing

Five days before John's birth, the Worcester County Convention met. Its members voted to reorganize the militia. British military officers, who reported directly to the royal governor, were dismissed. With tension growing between the American colonists and England, the mother country, every town was expected to form its own military force. One third of each town's men and boys between the ages of sixteen and sixty were to enlist.[6]

Massachusetts was a British colony ruled by King George III, who lived in England, and by a royal governor, who lived in Boston. All American colonists were expected to obey the laws passed by Parliament, Great Britain's legislative body. Because they were separated from Great Britain by the Atlantic Ocean, however, the American colonies had become used to making and obeying many of their own laws, without much interference.

So in the 1760s, when King George and Parliament began to pass laws that required the colonists to pay additional taxes, the colonists resisted because they had no representatives in Parliament. They claimed that taxation without representation was unjust. In 1766, the leaders of Leominster wrote a declaration that said, "we must, we can, and we will be free."[7]

For the most part, the colonists were successful in their efforts to avoid paying Parliament's taxes

**Taxation Without Representation**

Foreign wars had left England with many bills to pay. The British thought the American colonies should help make those payments, so King George and Parliament levied taxes, or special fees such as the Stamp Act of 1765. This act, which made it necessary to buy an official stamp for certain types of printed paper, including licenses, newspapers, and even playing cards, angered colonists. They thought of themselves as English citizens, with the same rights and privileges as those living in England. Most Englishmen had the right to vote on their own taxes, and the colonists expected that same right. But no one represented the Americans in Parliament, so the colonists complained that they were being taxed without representation.

until the spring of 1773. Then, Parliament put a tax on tea shipped to the colonies. Almost all colonists drank tea. They resisted strongly when their favorite beverage was taxed.

On December 16, 1773, men in Boston disguised as Mohawk Indians boarded a ship carrying tea from England. The Sons of Liberty, as the patriotic political group called itself, dumped thousands of pounds of British tea into Boston Harbor to prevent American colonists from paying the offensive tax. This event became known as the Boston Tea Party.

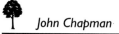 

To punish the city, the British closed Boston Harbor. No ship would be allowed to sail in or out until the city paid for the tea the patriots had destroyed. When the people of Boston refused, Parliament passed a law banning Massachusetts town meetings and the election of officials. The king also appointed an army general as the new governor of Massachusetts.

On August 22, 1774, Leominster citizens, dismayed by the plight of their Boston neighbors, wrote a letter of support. It said, "We must awaken and stir up every person to a thorough sense of the real certainty there now is of America being reduced to the most abject slavery and poverty. . . ."[8]

Soon the call went out for representatives from each colony to get together to plan ways to resist British laws. These men from the various British colonies met in Philadelphia, Pennsylvania, in September 1774, the month of John Chapman's birth. They were called the First Continental Congress. Delegates included such famous patriots as George Washington, Patrick Henry, John Adams, Thomas Jefferson, and John Hancock. They drafted and sent a letter to the king, requesting that Boston Harbor be reopened. They also passed a resolution that urged all colonies to stop trading with Great Britain, and called upon the people of Massachusetts to arm themselves.

## The War Begins

Nathaniel Chapman was one of the minutemen who answered the call of the First Continental Congress. He and other Leominster militiamen trained for more than nine months, preparing to defend their rights. On the night of April 18, 1775, the wait was over. Paul Revere and other messengers spread the alarm: "The British are coming! The British are coming!" Seven hundred of King George III's red-coated soldiers, stationed near Boston, were marching toward Lexington and Concord, Massachusetts. The Redcoats hoped to surprise the colonists, and raid their storehouse of guns and ammunition. When gunshots sounded the alarm on April 19, 1775, Leominster minutemen abandoned their chores and prepared for battle.

By the time the British soldiers reached Lexington, seventy minutemen were lined up on the town green, ready for battle. No one knows which side fired the first shot, but that shot is remembered today as "the shot heard round the world." It sent a clear message to England that the American colonists were determined to win their freedom.

Greatly outnumbered, the Lexington militia could not stop the Redcoats. Though they fought valiantly, when the skirmish ended, eight minutemen were dead. The British then marched confidently toward Concord. However, the colonists there had

*Though the minutemen pictured here seem to be well-outfitted, in reality few volunteers were dressed alike.*

a surprise for the Redcoats—more than three hundred minutemen were waiting, armed and ready.

During the battle at Concord's Old North Bridge, three Redcoats and two minutemen were killed before the British retreated. As the Redcoats marched back toward Boston, the American colonists continued the attack from behind trees and stone walls. Nearly three hundred British soldiers died or were wounded before they reached their ships in Boston Harbor.

The Leominster minutemen did not take part in the Battles of Lexington and Concord that marked the beginning of the American Revolution. By the time they arrived in Cambridge, near Boston, the surviving British soldiers had reached safety. But it was not long before Nathaniel Chapman had his own war experiences.

## Nathaniel Chapman, Soldier

Soon after the Battles of Lexington and Concord, the Second Continental Congress, another committee made up of representatives from each of the thirteen American colonies, met in Philadelphia. No longer simply organizing resistance to the British, the Congress now began to act as a governing body for the now united colonies. Determined to win freedom from British rule, the Congress selected George Washington as the Commander in Chief of the country's new armed forces, the Continental Army.

Nathaniel Chapman enlisted as a regular soldier. In June 1775, he participated in the Battle of Bunker Hill, part of the plan to drive the British from Boston and end the blockade of Boston Harbor. Although they won, the battle did not go well for the Redcoats. When it was over, they had eleven hundred casualties—dead, wounded, or missing soldiers. Some four hundred Americans died or were wounded.

Nathaniel's carpenter skills were needed by the army. He spent most of his time behind the lines,

fixing wagons and building forts. His efforts helped him receive a promotion to captain.

With most of the Leominster men and boys away fighting the war, the women did the farm work as well as housework. These strenuous chores were especially difficult for Elizabeth Chapman. She was expecting her third child and also had tuberculosis, an infectious disease of the lungs.[9]

On June 3, 1776, Elizabeth wrote a final message to her husband:

Loving Husband—

These lines come with my affectionate regards . . . hoping they will find you in health. . . . I am no better than I was when you left me but rather worse, and I should be very glad if you could come and see me for I want to see you. Our children are both well through the Divine goodness. . . . I rejoice to hear that you are well and I pray you may thus continue and in God's due time be returned in safety. . . . I desire your prayers for me . . . that I may so improve my remainder of life that I may answer the great end for which I was made, that I might glorify God here and finally come to the enjoyment of Him in a world of glory . . . and so I must bid you farewell and if it should be so ordered that I should not see you again, I hope we shall both be as happy as to spend an eternity of happiness together. So I conclude by subscribing myself, your
Ever loving and affectionate wife,
Elizabeth Chapman[10]

At the time Elizabeth sent her letter, the army was preparing its defenses against a British attack on New York. The British fleet sailed from Halifax,

**Family Treasure**
Time has saved just one personal memento of John Chapman's mother. Elizabeth's last brave letter to her husband was carefully treasured by Nathaniel and eventually given to his oldest daughter, Elizabeth. The original, handed down through the family, came to light 161 years later. When the letter was discovered, it belonged to a great-granddaughter of Chapman's older sister, who lived in Detroit, Michigan.[11]

Nova Scotia, in Canada, on June 10. One month later, British troops landed on Staten Island, New York. No one knows if Nathaniel Chapman tried to see his wife during these weeks of preparation, but it seems doubtful that his regiment would have allowed him to go home.

## Declaration and Death

On July 15, 1776, the citizens of Leominster celebrated the adoption of the Declaration of Independence. This document, drafted by Thomas Jefferson, declared the independence of the new United States of America from Great Britain. Leominster enthusiastically supported the idea and decided to follow the example of the Continental Congress by recording its own declaration of independence from British rule in the town record book.

However, the town's celebration did not lighten the mood of the Chapman family. Nathaniel was still away with the army. After giving birth to a son, Nathaniel, on June 26, Elizabeth lay in bed, overcome by tuberculosis. She died on July 18, 1776. Baby Nathaniel lived only a few weeks longer. John and his sister were left motherless.

# 3

# GROWING UP WITH A NEW COUNTRY

S ince no written record was left behind, historians can only guess what happened to John, not yet two, and his six-year-old sister, Elizabeth. They were too young to live alone in the family's house by the Nashua River. Their mother's parents owned a small frame house in Leominster, and the Chapman children may have lived with them until 1780.

Though the war did not end in an American victory until 1783, thirty-four-year-old Captain Nathaniel Chapman was released from the army on September 30, 1780. Some historians believe he was dismissed for mismanaging military supplies.[1] In any event, Nathaniel Chapman did not receive the

gift of land promised to all soldiers who fulfilled their wartime duty.

## A New Home

Two months before his army discharge, Nathaniel Chapman married again. His new bride, eighteen-year-old Lucy Cooley of Longmeadow, lived with her family near Springfield, Massachusetts, where the captain was stationed. After Nathaniel Chapman left the army, he and his wife rented a home from one of Lucy's relatives in her hometown.

While there is no written record, it is believed that John and Elizabeth Chapman lived with their father and his new bride. The family's little frame house, one of the oldest buildings in Longmeadow in 1780, was surrounded by wooded hills and open meadows. Trails outside the Chapmans' door meandered through forests and down to the Connecticut River. The area provided a wonderful playground for six-year-old John—an opportunity to learn about the forest and the wildlife that lived there.

It is likely that John spent much of his time outdoors, especially since the family home grew more crowded each year. Nathaniel and Lucy Chapman's first son, Nathaniel, was born in 1781. Abner was born in 1783. Then, at two-year intervals, Pierly, Lucy, Patty, Persis, Mary, Jonathan, Davis, and Sally arrived.

John probably went to church regularly with his family and may also have attended school.[2] Schools were quite different in the 1780s from today's modern classrooms. Lessons were learned from a hornbook, a piece of wood that looked something like a square ping-pong paddle. The alphabet was usually mounted on one side of the wooden form, and the Lord's Prayer on the other side. The text was protected from wear by a clear piece of animal horn, from which the hornbook got its name. Other printed sheets of text were mounted on the wood so students could practice reading out loud. Students often made so much noise reciting their lessons that neighbors complained about the schools.

One of John's half sisters remembered how he loved to read, borrowing books whenever possible.

### A Legendary Harvard Graduate

Because the details of John's schooling were completely lost, storytellers dreamed up imaginative tales to fill in the gaps. The story told most often is that John attended Harvard College outside Boston, Massachusetts, and graduated with honors.

This story, told again and again, claims that John's father was a Massachusetts clergyman and that John became a student of theology (religion) at Harvard. The story was probably an attempt to explain his intelligence. Although researchers searched for years to find proof that Chapman was a Harvard graduate, no student records for a John Chapman have ever been discovered.[3]

*Students learned to read from a hornbook. The text was protected by a clear covering made of animal horn.*

From facts known of his later life, it is believed that John was a good student, although he probably attended school for only a few years.

## An Independent, Expanding Country

While John was growing up in Longmeadow, the Americans continued their fight for independence from Great Britain. More than six years passed between the time the first shots were fired at Lexington and the British surrender to George Washington at Yorktown, Virginia, on October 19, 1781. John was nearly nine years old when the Treaty of Paris was signed two years later, on September 3, 1783, formally ending the war and extending the boundary of the United States westward to the Mississippi River.

Under British rule, settlement of American Indian territory west of the Allegheny Mountains had been discouraged, not to protect the lands of native tribes but to make it easier to control the valuable fur trade. Now with Great Britain out of the picture, even the threat of Indian attacks did not keep settlers from looking west, to the rich lands of the Northwest Territory. This was a huge area that eventually became the states of Ohio, Illinois, Indiana, Michigan, Wisconsin, and part of Minnesota. But it was more than the desire for land that drew pioneers west. They accepted the risks of frontier

life because of the opportunity to earn money. Many hoped to get rich.

The newly formed United States struggled with the best way to manage the new territory. In 1787, when John was twelve, the Continental Congress passed the Northwest Ordinance. It provided a fair way for new territories to become states. The land in the territory was divided into areas called townships. Groups of townships could become states when the population grew to more than sixty thousand. The system worked so well that it was used often as the nation grew.

The Northwest Ordinance guaranteed freedom of religion, habeas corpus (which forces authorities to bring an arrested person before a judge and either justify the arrest, or release the detained individual), and trial by jury. It also banned slavery and recognized the importance of education, requiring each township to set aside land for public schools.

Also in 1787, the autobiographical account of *The Adventures of Colonel Daniel Boon* [*sic*] was published in the *American Magazine*. The article described how frontiersman Daniel Boone had opened the Kentucky Territory, cut the Wilderness Road, and helped settlers establish Boonesborough, Kentucky. In 1775, the American frontiersman was one of the first to blaze a trail over the Appalachian Mountains, a range that separated the Atlantic coastline from central North America. He helped

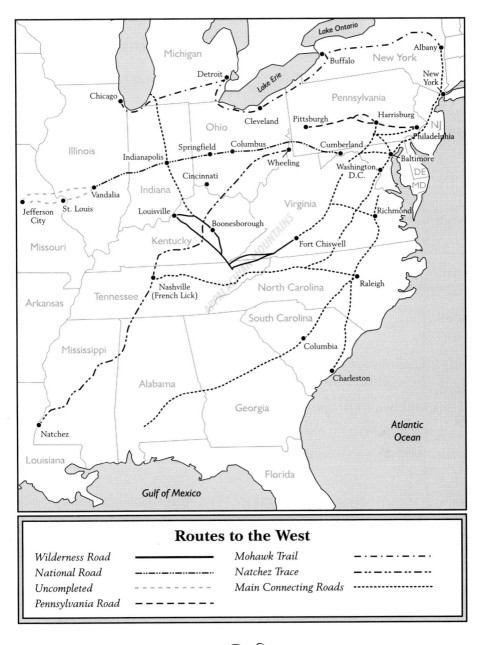

## Routes to the West

| | | | |
|---|---|---|---|
| Wilderness Road | ———————— | Mohawk Trail | —··—··—··—·· |
| National Road | —··—··—··—·· | Natchez Trace | —··—··—··—·· |
| Uncompleted | — — — — — | Main Connecting Roads | ·············· |
| Pennsylvania Road | — — — — — | | |

*This map shows the routes most early settlers followed to the West, which is now the Midwest.*

open a route that thousands of settlers would later follow west.

Many of John's Longmeadow neighbors piled their belongings into big wooden-wheeled wagons and headed out on the main road from Boston and Springfield, Massachusetts, to Albany, New York, and points west. But in 1787, John was too young to follow. He could only watch, wait, and learn.

## Learning a Trade

During this time, boys of fourteen could work for wages. However, they did not get to keep what they earned. Laws required that the wages be given to the boys' fathers. To help with the family's expenses, Nathaniel Chapman probably hired John, his oldest son, out to local farmers to work in their fields and orchards. Some early stories even suggest that John was apprenticed as an orchard keeper. This is not unlikely, since the Chapmans lived in an apple-growing section of Massachusetts. It is quite possible that John's first lessons in how to plant and care for apple trees were learned in a Longmeadow orchard.

The apple tree was extremely important to pioneer communities. It was the easiest fruit tree to grow and it had many important uses. Apples were one of the crops used throughout the year. Hardier varieties provided a family with fruit from early summer until the following spring. Cold apples buried in late autumn would keep for several months underground. Bushels of apples were dried in the fall until they were needed to make sauces. Many more bushels were cooked to make gallons of apple butter, which lasted for months.

In late autumn, apples not cooked down for butter or stored for the winter were taken to cider presses to make juice. Every pioneer family used many barrels of apple cider. In autumn the freshly

*In late autumn, apples not cooked down for butter or stored underground were hauled by the wagonload to the cider presses to make juice. Every pioneer family used many barrels of apple cider.*

squeezed drink was delicious; it grew increasingly appealing to some as it began to ferment into hard cider, an alcoholic drink many frontier men enjoyed. For the frontier woman, cider and vinegar were two basic flavorings and preservatives.

## Go West, Young Man

In 1794, a treaty was signed with the Seneca Nation, six American Indian tribes that claimed territory in western New York State and northern Pennsylvania. By the fall of 1797, the Holland Land Company began offering large tracts of land at low prices in northwestern Pennsylvania. Reports that the land was fertile persuaded many white settlers to leave the rocky, overworked soil of Massachusetts to move west.

It was about this time that John Chapman, now an independent young man of twenty-two or twenty-three, must have decided to strike out on his own. Some stories say Chapman traveled alone. Others suggest that his half brother Nathaniel went with him.

There is no record of Chapman's path west. It is likely he started out along the Boston Post Road, the main route from Boston to New York City. It crossed the Connecticut River at Springfield. Emigrants passed west along that road daily. From New York City, he may have traveled south to Philadelphia, then taken the Pennsylvania Road overland to Lancaster and Harrisburg, then across the Allegheny Mountains and into Pittsburgh. The trip would have taken three or four weeks of hard travel. While details are not known, it seems likely that Pittsburgh was one of Chapman's first stops as he migrated west.

From the Pittsburgh area, one story suggests that the Chapman brothers followed the Allegheny River to Olean Creek near the New York state line. They were searching for an uncle, but unfortunately, he had moved.[4]

Though we can only guess about John Chapman's route, we do know he carried with him ideas about orchards and apples. Perhaps these ideas were a bit of his New England home that he could carry west, since "in Massachusetts, apple pie was a favorite dessert— eaten not only at supper but also for breakfast."[5]

The truth of the matter is, though storytellers have invented many probable and imaginative tales about John Chapman, no documented records exist today that tell us about John's life between his birth in Leominster in 1774, and his first recorded appearance in the area around Pittsburgh in 1797.

4

# BLOWN IN BY A BLIZZARD

Johnn Chapman began to leave footprints on the frontier during the 1790s, but his trail was faint and nearly impossible to trace. Many stories place the young man in Pittsburgh early in the decade, suggesting that Chapman worked in the boat yards, building flat boats used by pioneers to float west along the Ohio River. There may be some truth to these tales, since in 1794, a John Chapman took an oath of allegiance to the new United States federal government in Washington County, a few miles southwest of Pittsburgh.[1]

## Chapman's First Western Appearance

The first reliable record of Chapman's living in the western wilderness of Pennsylvania was written in 1853. According to Judge Lansing Wetmore, Chapman arrived in October 1797 during an early snowstorm. He was on his way to the newly founded town of Warren, Pennsylvania, which consisted of only one log building.

Wetmore's account places Chapman about halfway across the state, just below the New York line, in a wilderness that had not been widely explored. In this area, the level land that forms the Allegheny plateau heaves up into ridges, raising the general elevation to over twenty-five hundred feet. Streams form within a short distance of each other, and flow north to the Genessee River and the Great Lakes, east to the Susquehanna River and the Atlantic Ocean, and west to the Allegheny, and eventually into the Gulf of Mexico.

Wetmore's story is not an eyewitness account. The judge did not arrive in the area until 1815. However, he recorded stories told by the first homesteaders in the territory. He also claimed to have seen what was left of one of Chapman's first apple tree orchards. Another sign that supports Wetmore's accounts of local history is that the name "Johnny Appleseed" does not appear in any of his reports. Possibly the judge never heard the nickname, or maybe he did not realize that Johnny Appleseed was the same man who planted apple trees in Warren.

Wetmore's report supports the fact the Chapman was more than a kind man growing apple trees for settlers out of the goodness of his heart. He was a businessman. According to the judge, Chapman left the Warren area when he discovered the limited demand for fruit trees and "went [about fifty miles farther south] to Franklin, where he established another nursery."[2]

Hard evidence that seems to confirm Chapman and his fifteen-year-old brother Nathaniel's presence in Franklin about 1798 is found in trading post ledgers. Those records carried the names of John and Nathaniel Chapman between 1797 and 1800.[3] However, no one can prove that the John Chapman listed on those ledgers was the same person later known as Johnny Appleseed.

## Seedlings and Settlements

It took several years for apple trees to bear fruit. Chapman's plan was to have seedlings ready and waiting to sell to the first settlers in the area. He gathered apple seeds from cider mills near the Pittsburgh area and packed them in burlap sacks. Sometimes, he carried the large bags on his back. At other times, he used a horse. Then he headed west to Franklin, Pennsylvania, about fifty miles south of Warren.

Newly open to settlement, Franklin was one of the best points to meet new settlers. There was

### A Legendary Love

A tale of lost love is another story often repeated as part of the Johnny Appleseed myth. The beginnings of this yarn, found in recollections recorded only ten or fifteen years after his death, contain references to an unhappy love affair—though none can be documented.

In the most common story, John Chapman falls in love with Dorothy Durand, but their families are bitter enemies because of differing religious beliefs. At some point, Dorothy's family moves west, separating the sweethearts. But Chapman will not give up. Soon he heads west to search for Dorothy. He eventually finds the Durands, but then the tale takes a sorrowful turn. The young man learns that his beloved has died—of a broken heart.

Though the girl's name is not always the same in the different versions of the legend, several authors repeated similar events. Each of these stories claims that, "many years later, John returned to plant apple blossoms on her grave."[4]

plenty of unclaimed land—wilderness spots where Chapman could plant patches of apple seeds. Because many landowners actually lived far away in cities along the east coast, Chapman did not bother to obtain a deed or lease the land. He simply planted his seeds in the rich soil along French Creek just above the town. Soon his young trees were ready for

the thousands of families headed for the Ohio country, where fertile land cost one to two dollars per acre. Settlers who purchased property through the Ohio Land Company had to plant fifty apple trees during the first year of settlement. The company believed that fruit trees gave the owner a feeling of home and stability.

In 1800, Franklin, Pennsylvania, was a trading center populated by only ten families. As new settlers arrived in the area, they would replenish their supplies and ask for directions before striking out to claim land. The census of 1800 showed only 161 men in the entire area that stretched up French Creek. At least sixty-four were single men. Some were trappers and traders. Many were young men trying to follow the legal requirements to earn title to a one-hundred-acre farm. While guarding against others who might jump, or steal, his claim, each young man had to clear the land, raise a crop, build a shelter, and prove his intent to stay, if he hoped to gain title to his property.

John Chapman's name was reported as a resident of Franklin by the federal census in April 1801. The report shows that the twenty-six-year-old was living alone. He was listed under the category Head of Family, the term used to describe bachelors.

The fact that Chapman did not hold legally recorded titles to any land in Pennsylvania makes it very difficult to verify the sites of his early nurseries.

County histories, which provide the most reliable source of information, locate one of Chapman's orchards, possibly his first, on Big Brokenstraw Creek near Warren, and another on French Creek near Franklin. He tended both nurseries from about 1797 to 1804, traveling from one to the other to care for the trees and to sell his seedlings. Other sources suggest that Chapman had more nurseries in the area, but the information is not reliable.[5] It is believed that all his nurseries were located near the westward routes used by settlers.

It is likely that Chapman spent the years between 1797 and 1800 along French Creek, working a land claim. The friendly Seneca and Munsee Indians still lived in the area. He may have learned many of his wilderness survival skills from them. Chapman moved freely among the Indians, living as they did. He was one of the rare white men who were respected and accepted by the American Indians.[6]

## Mad Anthony Wayne and the Battle of Fallen Timbers

Though relationships with the Munsee and Seneca tribes were peaceful in western Pennsylvania, Indian trouble prevented settlement farther west. In 1790, Congress sent troops in response to appeals by new western settlers for protection. Brigadier General Josiah Harmar's orders were to punish the Wabash

and Miami Indians for their raids on flatboats and canoes floating downriver. However, the Indians, led by Chief Little Turtle, soundly defeated Harmar's army on October 22, 1790, and a second regiment led by General Arthur St. Clair in November 1791, near the area now known as Fort Recovery, Ohio.

Fearing that Great Britain would take this opportunity to invade the United States from Canada, President George Washington sent more troops under the command of General Anthony Wayne. Wayne moved his forces to the Cincinnati area in the summer of 1793. There, he waited for orders to

**Mad Anthony Wayne**

Several stories try to explain how Anthony Wayne earned his nickname, "Mad" Anthony Wayne. One version claims that Wayne was named by Jemy the Rover, who served as Wayne's principal spy during the American Revolution. During 1781, Jemy's behavior became inappropriate. Wayne ordered him whipped twenty-nine times. The spy is said to have exclaimed, "Anthony is mad, stark mad," then repeated again and again, "Mad Anthony Wayne."[7] However, most historians believe Wayne actually earned the nickname because of his reckless courage in the face of the enemy.

*After Mad Anthony Wayne defeated the Indians at the Battle of Fallen Timbers, white settlers could safely homestead the Northwest Territory.*

attack. The president still hoped to settle problems with the Indians without further fighting.

By the fall of 1793, attempts to negotiate a settlement had failed. The United States would not prevent its citizens from settling beyond the Ohio River. And the Indians refused to recognize the claims white intruders made upon their lands. On September 11, 1793, Wayne was told to attack. In December, Wayne led his troops north to the place where the Indians had defeated St. Clair. There, Wayne built Fort Recovery. The following June, the fort was attacked.

Though greatly outnumbered by the Indian soldiers, according to one historian, "the well-trained dragoons and riflemen within the professionally built fort held out against overwhelming odds. The Indians were forced to retreat."[8]

Wayne and his troops continued traveling north, building Fort Defiance (now Defiance, Ohio), in August 1794. About fifty miles away, thirteen hundred Indians prepared for battle outside Fort Miami, where the British still had a stronghold near present-day Toledo, Ohio. Hoping to negotiate, Wayne sent a message to the four tribes. But the tribes would not surrender.

On August 20, 1794, Wayne's troops attacked the Indians at Fallen Timbers, just south of the Toledo area. The battle lasted less than an hour. The defeated tribesmen fled.

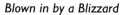

The American soldiers burned several nearby American Indian villages and destroyed their food supplies. Then General Wayne moved southeast into Indiana Territory and built Fort Wayne where the St. Joseph and the St. Mary rivers meet to form the Maumee River.

After a hungry winter, the defeated tribes signed the Treaty of Greenville in August 1795. Peace was restored, but the Wyandot, Delaware, Shawnee, Ottawa, Chippewa, Pattawatima, Miami, Eel River, Wea, Kickapoo, Piankeshaw and Kaskaskia tribes

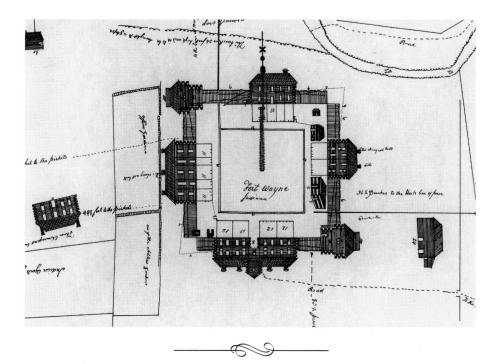

*This sketch shows the historic fort built by General Anthony Wayne.*

had to give up rights to all their land in Ohio, except for the northwest corner.[9]

With Wayne's decisive victory at Fallen Timbers, white settlers could now safely homestead the Northwest Territory, and the population grew quickly. By 1799, more than five thousand free males lived in the territory—enough to give the settlers the right to elect their own representatives. Then in 1803, with a population of more than 11 million people, Ohio became a state.

## Moving on

By 1804, the Pennsylvania wilderness was becoming too heavily populated for John Chapman. His half brother Nathaniel had gone west into Ohio and settled near the town of Marietta. Chapman's father, his wife, and their younger children had also moved from Longmeadow to the Marietta area.

Two legal documents add to Chapman's story. In 1804, Chapman signed IOUs for one hundred dollars each—one to the children of his sister, Elizabeth Rudd, and one to Nathaniel Chapman. It is not clear whether this Nathaniel was John's father or his half brother.

To whom Chapman actually owed money is not as important as what the IOU said: "I promise to pay Nathaniel Chapman . . . the sum of one hundred dollars in land or apple trees."[10] This was the first

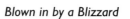

written evidence of John Chapman's interest in apple trees.

Historians speculate that Chapman used these funds to pay for a move. Whatever the purpose, Chapman did head west about this time into the Ohio Territory, which was to become the birthplace of his legend.

# 5

# ACROSS THE NORTHWEST TERRITORY

In the early 1800s, as John Chapman became a frequent and welcome visitor to settlers' homes in the Ohio Territory, pioneers began to tell tales of the orchardist. Dr. E. Bonar McLaughlin recorded one such memory in his *Pioneer Directory and Scrapbook*: "Chapman often visited at my Uncle John Stewart's . . . and my Uncle Andrew Thompson's. My recollection . . . is that he was about five feet, seven inches tall, straight as an arrow, slim and wiry as a cat."[1]

At this point, he was most likely clean-shaven, although he grew a beard in later life. Another story suggests that Chapman had sunken cheeks, a small mouth, and an upturned nose.[2] Many remembered his long dark hair and his dark, almost black, eyes that sparkled brightly.[3]

In the 1800s, most frontiersmen wore pantaloons made of blue cloth or deerskin, a handkerchief tied on their heads, deerskin moccasins, and a blanket coat secured at the waist with a belt. A butcher's knife and a leather pouch to hold tobacco, pipe, flint, and steel hung from the belt.

Chapman dressed in cast-off garments, many of which he took as payment for apple trees. He even made his own shirts by cutting holes for his head and arms in a coffee sack. He claimed it was "as good clothing as any man need wear."[4]

He may have worn a wide-brimmed felt hat, or one he made himself with a pasteboard bill much like the one on a baseball cap. But there is no evidence that he used a tin pot for a hat, as legends often claim.

He rarely wore shoes, even in the coldest weather. Sometimes, for long journeys, he made a crude pair of sandals. Other times he wore shoes he happened to find—possibly hiking along with a boot on one foot and a moccasin on the other. His appearance was very strange, even by frontier standards. Some tried to explain his unusual behavior by claiming that, as a young man, he had been kicked in the head by a horse.

Both men and women of the time frequently went without shoes in summer, although they did

*This portrait of John Chapman was drawn several years after his death by someone who had once seen him.*

wear moccasins or other shoes during the winter. Most people could not tolerate pain and cold like Chapman. Many claimed that he did not even feel the cold when he walked barefoot over ice and snow. His feet were so callused that one settler said any rattlesnake that tried to bite him on the foot would die.[5]

## Along River Roads

John Chapman said he was twenty-six when he first ventured into Ohio in 1801.[6] He arrived with a horse-load of apple seeds, which he planted along Licking Creek, east of present-day Columbus, Ohio. Only three white families lived in Licking County at the time. One of the settlers, John Larabee, made his home in the hollow of a huge sycamore tree until he could build a log cabin.[7]

For the next five years, there was no record of Chapman in this territory, although he probably traveled back and forth between his Pennsylvania and Ohio nurseries. In the spring of 1806, a Jefferson County settler saw a strange craft floating down the Ohio River along the boundary between West Virginia and Ohio. Chapman had lashed two canoes together to carry his load of apple seeds.[8] Historians believe the thirty-one-year-old was headed for Marietta, Ohio.

The young man's father, Captain Nathaniel Chapman, had recently moved to that river town

with his wife, Lucy, five daughters, and five sons. John Chapman may have stopped briefly to visit with his family. Then he paddled up the Muskingum River, to the Walhonding, or White Woman Creek. From there, he traveled up the Mohican to the source of the Black Fork.

At every inviting spot along the way, Chapman would throw a bag of apple seeds over his shoulder, walk to a fertile spot, and plant his seeds. His final task was to build a fence to keep out cattle and deer. Then he would move on, leaving his seed to sprout and grow into seedlings.

Though his planting routine may have appeared haphazard, Chapman knew exactly what he was doing. The first place people settled in new territory was generally near a stream. He planted his wilderness groves with these customers in mind and rarely made a poor choice. Many towns sprang up near sites he selected.

Chapman's trip ended in central Ohio, an area newly opened for settlement, now part of Ashland and Richland counties. He had arrived before most settlers and was assured of steady business, since land companies required homesteaders to plant fruit trees. Chapman was not the only nurseryman to recognize this great opportunity. In fact, he cannot even claim to be the first, because several other nurseries were already established in the new state of Ohio. Chapman's orchards, however, were significant

*The last surviving apple tree believed to have been planted by Chapman is on the Algeo Farm near Savannah, Ohio. It still blooms and bears fruit every year.*

because the sites were selected so carefully and because he planted more trees than anyone else. Almost every community in central Ohio can point to a spot along a creek or on a sunny hillside, and claim that Johnny Appleseed once planted seeds there. While many of these claims are unfounded, biographer Robert Price was able to document the sites of thirty of Chapman's Ohio orchards.

Though no proof exists today to verify the sites of other orchards, Chapman seemed to sow seeds wherever he went. It might have been his way of thanking a pioneer family for food, shelter, or a bit of conversation around the fireplace.

In 1806, Chapman traditionally charged a "fippenny bit" for a seedling apple tree, or about six and a half cents.[9] If a buyer had no cash, Chapman would accept clothing, a bit of cornmeal, or even the promise to pay in the future. He also reportedly gave trees to needy families.

## To Market, to Market

At this time, travel was easier by water than by overland routes for settlers crossing the Appalachian Mountains. Streams cut through the hills at their lowest points, forming valleys that offered good farmland. It is not surprising that settlements grew up along riverbanks.

Water travel was also the easier way to bring goods to market. Settlers in the Northwest Territory

**A Diet of Nuts and Berries**

Because Chapman was a gentle man with a great respect for all living creatures, he did not believe in hunting. Instead, he often made meals of the nuts and berries he could gather.

He may also have carried journey bread, a typical food used by American Indians when they traveled. It was nutritious and stayed fresh for a long time. The first step to make journey bread was to boil green corn, still on the ears, until it was half-done. After the ears had dried in the sun for a few days, the corn was browned in hot ashes. Then it was pounded into fine meal and finally mixed with maple sugar.[10]

preferred to float their produce nearly two thousand miles down the Ohio and Mississippi rivers to New Orleans, rather than risk going overland to the east coast. This meant farmers needed produce that could survive such a long trip without spoiling. Apples held up well during travel and could also be shipped as cider and apple butter.

## Welcome Guest

Chapman was always treated respectfully by frontiersmen. Even the boys of the settlements did not make fun of this strange character. Often described as a kind, quiet, likeable man, he was a welcome guest in the homes of Ohio settlers.

If invited to have supper with a family, Chapman would never eat until he was sure that the children had enough. He never drank alcoholic beverages excessively, did not drink coffee or tea, and did not use tobacco.

After supper, he would gather the boys and girls around him and tell them stories, like the one about the time he was paddling along a partially frozen stream. As large chunks of ice floated by Chapman and his canoe, he noticed that the ice seemed to be moving faster than he could paddle. Hoping to reach

*This building, now used as a storage shed, is the original farmhouse where Chapman visited the great-grandparents of the Algeos, owners of the farm where his last surviving tree stands.*

his destination more quickly, Chapman put his canoe up on top of a piece of moving ice. The plan might have worked, except that he fell asleep. When he woke up, he discovered that he had floated miles past his destination.

Chapman always had pieces of colorful cloth to give as gifts to little girls. Before bedtime, he might

### A Legendary Friend

Legends about Johnny Appleseed include one about his jabbering to the squirrels until they came and took nuts out of his hand:

> He whistled so robins flew to him, thinking they heard their mates. He gobbled until all the wild turkey flocked in a crowd around him. Even shy quail came out of the meadows in answer to his call. Fawns sometimes followed Johnny, so he had to speak harshly to make them go back to their mothers.[11]

Another time, he is said to have put out the fire he built near a hollow log, and slept in the snow, because he found that a bear and her cubs were inside the log and he did not want to disturb them.[12]

These tales are pure legend, but it is certain Chapman was a friend to wild animals. Stories tell how he refused to kill a bee that had stung him. He even put out his campfire one night when mosquitoes were flying into it, saying, "God forbid that I should build a fire for my comfort which should be the means of destroying any of His creatures."[13]

*Chapman was a gentle man and a friend to all animals.*

lead the family in prayer. Chapman preferred to sleep in the barn or woodshed, or out in the backyard under an apple tree. Only in the worst winter weather would he stay inside the house and bed down in front of the warm fireplace.

Though no one really knows when or how Chapman first became known by his nickname, many pioneer families have passed down stories from one generation to another, recalling early frontier life in Ohio, Johnny Appleseed's visits to their homes, and the gifts he left behind.

By 1806, Chapman was selling apple trees in Mount Vernon, Ohio, from seeds he had planted on land owned by other farmers. The owners tended the trees in return for a share of the new seedlings.

Three years later, Chapman bought two town lots in Mount Vernon. The lots were purchased as sites for more orchards.[14] Chapman prepared to make his business more permanent in strategic locations as settlers continued to pour into the territory.

While all the new settlers were good business for Chapman, they were bad news for the American Indians, who were still clinging to land in Ohio and other parts of the Northwest Territory. Trouble was brewing across the land.

# 6

# THE WAR
# OF 1812

When John Chapman first moved to the Ohio Territory, there were far more American Indians living there than white settlers. However, by the time many of his seeds had matured into fruit-bearing apple trees, the population of homesteaders was growing rapidly.

Indian trails crisscrossed the area near Mansfield and Mount Vernon, Ohio. Two Delaware Indian villages were located not far from the frontier towns. The largest consisted of sixty homes and a bark council house.[1] For the most part, the tribes lived peacefully with their new neighbors.

Chapman traveled freely across Indian territory in the state's northwest corner, planting his seeds. He spoke the Indians' languages and often stayed in their villages.[2] The orchardist could see how quickly the land claimed by the Delaware, Wyandot, and Shawnee tribes was being settled by whites. Chapman was sympathetic to the loss of the American Indians' hunting grounds, and tried to help. He planted apple seeds near the tribal villages and taught the Indians how to cultivate the trees.

The Indians were amazed by Chapman's ability to endure pain. He could stick pins and needles into his feet without flinching. He would sear or burn cuts and sores with a piece of red-hot iron to sterilize them.[3]

The Indians regarded Chapman as a great medicine man. He willingly shared his knowledge of the healing power of herbs with friends, no matter what the color of their skin. As he wandered through the woods, he gathered horehound, catnip, pennyroyal, ginseng, goldenseal, wood bitney, and dog fennel—all wild plants used as medicines.

Many Indians believed Chapman was blessed by the Great Spirit, the god they worshiped. They often allowed him to listen to their council meetings.[4] This information sometimes helped Chapman prevent trouble between the Indians and the white settlers. But when the British, who still had forts near Lake Erie in Michigan Territory, offered weapons

to the American Indians and encouraged them to attack settlers, even Chapman could not prevent the bloodshed that followed.

## Tecumseh and the Prophet

In the early 1800s, Shawnee Chief Tecumseh, who had refused to sign the Treaty of Greenville in 1795 and give up his tribe's rights to lands in the Ohio Territory, tried to unite the tribes of the northwestern frontier. He hoped to prevent white homesteaders from claiming more of the Indians' hunting grounds. Americans had earned Tecumseh's hatred when he was young. He had watched white settlers who wanted Shawnee lands kill his father and older brothers. The chief realized that the whites would eventually take over all Indian lands unless the tribes formed a strong alliance.

Tecumseh traveled thousands of miles, preaching his message to the American Indian tribes. By 1808, he had attracted many followers. Shawnee, Wyandot, Kickapoo, Delaware, and Ottawa joined Tecumseh and his brother, the Prophet, at their new encampment called Prophetstown. The village was located along the Tippecanoe River in what is now northwestern Indiana.

The white settlers in the Indiana Territory became increasingly fearful of Tecumseh's power. They knew the Shawnee chief would try to drive them out when he felt strong enough. They asked the territorial governor, General William Henry Harrison, for protection before it was too late.

In November 1811, Harrison and a thousand soldiers advanced to the banks of the Tippecanoe River across from Prophetstown. The general had chosen the perfect time to make his move. Tecumseh was visiting tribes in the south and was not expected to return for months. Before he left, he had warned the Prophet, his second-in-command, not to fight the whites. If soldiers came, his brother was supposed to guard the town and promise anything to avoid a battle.

The Prophet, who had accurately predicted an eclipse of the sun, also claimed to receive messages from the Great Spirit, revealing the future. He ignored Tecumseh's orders and prepared for battle, promising his two thousand soldiers an easy victory. He told them that he had put a spell on the white soldiers, making them too weak to defend themselves. His spell also supposedly made the Indians invulnerable to enemy bullets. The Prophet ordered his band to kill Harrison, the white leader who rode a gray horse.

On the morning of November 7, a sentry posted near Harrison's camp spotted Indians and opened fire. Normally, the Indians would have moved forward slowly, hiding behind trees and large rocks. However, the Prophet's vision had foretold an easy victory, so the Indians charged the camp. Harrison's

troops easily drove them back three times. The Indians discovered that the Prophet, who lacked his brother Tecumseh's great leadership abilities, had deserted them, as it soon became clear that his vision was false. They panicked and fled. Later that day, Harrison ordered Prophetstown burned to the ground. Tecumseh was enraged by his brother's defeat and turned to the British for aid.

## The War of 1812

Less than forty years after the American colonies declared their independence from Great Britain and started the Revolutionary War, the two countries were again at odds. This time the dispute was primarily over America's freedom of the seas.

**Legendary Hero**

Storytellers have made John Chapman, or Johnny Appleseed, a hero of the Battle of Tippecanoe. One account claims Chapman served as a mediator and scout. During the battle, he was said to have taken care of those who were wounded or dying. The account even claims that two bullets struck Chapman, but the Bible he carried over his heart saved his life. This Tippecanoe episode about Chapman is fiction. Possibly, it was inspired by Chapman's nighttime trip to warn Ohio settlers of possible Indian attack, which occurred about a year later.

In 1804, when Napoleon Bonaparte, emperor of France, challenged Great Britain's control of the seas, the United States got caught in the middle. Each country claimed the right to seize any foreign ships that traded with its enemy.

The situation grew worse in 1807, when the British passed the Orders in Council. The orders stated that ships of neutral nations trading with European countries must pass through British ports and have British licenses. The United States, now the largest neutral trading nation, was outraged. Many American ships refused to get licenses. Instead, they tried to get around British and French blockades. In retaliation, the British seized American-operated ships that did not comply, and forced American sailors to serve in the British Navy.

President James Madison tried to resolve differences with England, but failed. Pressured by the War Hawks, members of Congress who were ready to fight, the president finally sent an ultimatum to Great Britain: Stop the search and seizure of American ships or face war. On June 18, 1812, the Congress of the United States declared war.

For the next two and a half years, British and American ships exchanged fire on the Atlantic Ocean and on Lakes Champlain and Erie. The war even reached Washington, D.C., the nation's capital, when the British briefly occupied the new city. Many buildings, including the President's House,

**An Unnecessary War**

If today's communications technology had been available two hundred years ago, the War of 1812 might have been prevented. Two days before Congress declared war, the British Parliament agreed to stop the search and seizure of American ships. But in those days, messages took weeks to sail across the ocean. The war had already begun by the time the message reached President Madison and Congress.

now known as the White House, were damaged by fires the British started.

## Wartime Scout

Most battles of the War of 1812 were fought at sea. However, another issue was of great concern to the settlers in the western territories. There, the dispute was over the border separating the United States from Canada, which was then a British colony. Some American Indians, like Tecumseh, sided with the British, who encouraged them to resist white settlers in the Northwest Territory.

The Delaware Indians who lived in the Mansfield area became an immediate concern to settlers. Most Indians left the area for their own safety, but families north of Mansfield still felt threatened. They asked John Chapman to go north to Lake Erie at least once a week and warn them of possible danger from the British and Indians. The nurseryman who had scouted the area while planting apple seeds knew the territory well.

Tension was high in the area in August, after Detroit fell to the British.[5] When one settler was killed in early September, the others feared for their lives. Chapman volunteered to warn others in the area, making his legendary journey for help. Though no attack came that night, a few days later, bad news reached Mansfield.

Eight miles to the east, a small band of Indians killed a settler, his wife, his daughter, and a neighbor who had tried to warn the family. Settlers in the region immediately fled to the nearest forts.

However, only a few days later, a minister who lived near Mansfield wanted to go home with his family. He had faith in his longtime friendship with the Delaware, and was sure they would not harm him or his family. The garrison commander sent soldiers with the reverend, his wife, and their children to ensure their safety. They could not prevent what happened next. A band of forty-five Delaware warriors attacked the troops and the family on September 15. After five hours of fighting, the minister and three of the soldiers were dead. Others were wounded. The raiding party also burned cabins in the valley. Most families were afraid to return to remote areas around Mansfield after the raid.[6]

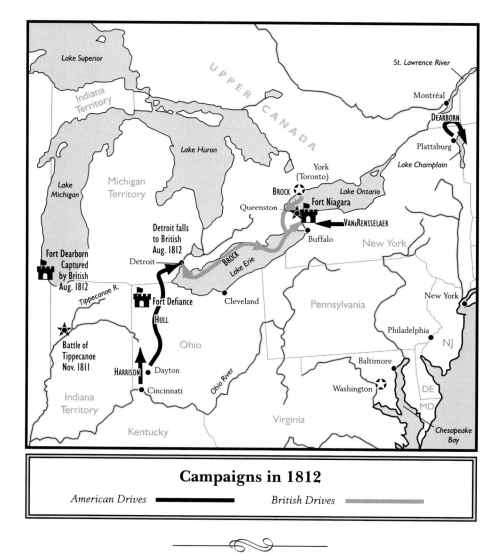

## Campaigns in 1812

American Drives ■■■■■■  British Drives ▬▬▬▬▬

*The War of 1812 was fought mainly on the seas and in the western territories of the United States.*

The Indian opposition ended on October 5, 1813, north of Lake Erie at the Battle of the Thames. British troops led by General Henry Proctor and American Indians under the leadership of Tecumseh confronted a regiment led by General William Henry Harrison, who had also commanded the American forces at the Battle of Tippecanoe. Though the battle lasted only a few minutes, hundreds of Indians died, including Tecumseh.

The signing of the Treaty of Ghent ended the War of 1812 officially on Christmas Eve, 1814. Despite several fierce battles, neither side gained much from the war. The treaty did not address boundary lines between the United States and Canada, or the search and seizure of American ships and sailors. But the war did show the character of John Chapman. Throughout the war, Chapman devoted his energy to protecting his friends and trying to pacify the Indians.[7]

## Back to Business

Once peace was restored, Chapman began to buy more property for his orchards. By 1815, he owned six hundred forty acres, including lots in Mount Vernon, one in Mansfield, and three hundred acres of farmland in neighboring counties. Sometimes he paid for the land with the promise of apple trees. More often, Chapman paid cash.

*Shawnee Chief Tecumseh refused to sign the Treaty of Greenville in 1795, which would give up his tribe's rights to lands in the Ohio Territory. He was killed during the War of 1812.*

He later leased nine hundred additional acres in other parts of the state. These agreements, made with the state of Ohio, required payments of $19.20 each year.

While some details of Chapman's business practice have been revealed by scraps of information gathered by historians, little is known of the orchardist's personal life. There is a documented fact from this time period that does shed some light on his personal convictions. In 1816, Chapman, a patriot who had great faith in his country, presented a Fourth of July address in Huron County.[8] It was said that the orchardist spoke with great power on subjects that interested him. In fact, he could hold an apple in his hand and charm his listeners with his discussion of the fruit.[9] This speaking ability would help Chapman plant seeds of another kind.

# 7

# SPREADING THE GOOD WORD

John Chapman was forty-two years old before his story was first told in print. However, the story was not about his life as a nurseryman or frontier hero, but about his work as a missionary who shared his religious beliefs with other settlers in the wilderness:

> There is in the western country a very extraordinary missionary of the New Jerusalem. A man . . . [who] goes barefooted, can sleep anywhere, in house or out of house, and lives upon the coarsest and most scanty fare. He has actually thawed the ice with his bare feet.
>
> He procures what books he can of the New Church; travels into the remote settlements, and lends them wherever he can find readers, and sometimes divides a book into two or three parts for more extensive distribution and usefulness.
>
> This man for years past has been in the employment of . . . sowing apple seeds and rearing nurseries.[1]

These excerpts were printed in a report of the Manchester Society in England in 1817. The report suggests that Chapman was well-known by several members of the Church of the New Jerusalem living in communities east of the Allegheny Mountains. Several letters written between 1817 and 1822 by a prominent Philadelphia Swedenborgian, William

### The Swedenborgian Church

Emanuel Swedenborg, whose theological writings were the foundation for the Church of the New Jerusalem, also called the Swedenborgian Church, was born on January 19, 1688, in Stockholm, Sweden. He became a learned scientist. For the last twenty-seven years of his life, he devoted his time to theological, or religious, writings.

The Swedenborgian Church was formed in London, fifteen years after Swedenborg's death. The church encouraged a spirit of inquiry (questioning), respect for different points of view, and acceptance of others with different traditions. Swedenborg's writings reflected his view of a loving God. He said, "All religion relates to life, and the life of religion is to do good."[2] He believed that leading a useful life was the best way to worship God.

It is believed that an English plantation owner introduced Swedenborg's teachings to America in 1784, through a series of lectures in Philadelphia.

Schlatter, also suggest that Chapman was known in the area.

Schlatter, an importer and wholesaler of dry goods in Philadelphia, corresponded with Chapman for more than seven years. The businessman also supplied at least part of the church literature that the orchardist shared with pioneer families in the West. This fact was verified in a letter Schlatter wrote to the pastor of the New Church Society in Wheeling, West Virginia:

> I have sent some books to Mr. Chapman, do you know him and has he received the Books, he travels about in Ohio and has much to do with appletrees; I am told he is a singular man but greatly in love with the New Church doctrines and takes great pains in deseminating [sic] them.[3]

Though its not known for sure when the nickname Johnny Appleseed replaced Chapman's given name, it was first recorded in a letter written by William Schlatter to a minister in Virginia: "They call him John Appleseed out there [Mansfield, Ohio]. If you do not know his history I will give it to you in my next [letter] if you desire, as it is interesting."[4]

## Swedenborgian Missionary

Chapman was probably one of the earliest New Church converts, or believers, in America. Even by 1817, when the organization held its first General Convention in Philadelphia, there were fewer than four hundred followers of the faith in the United States. Chapman was one of the first to carry the Swedenborgian message into the Northwest Territory.

In 1818, a Methodist minister named Silas Ensign moved to Richland County, Ohio. He built a cabin a few miles away from Mansfield and soon became a confirmed believer of the New Church doctrine. The young minister organized a group of Swedenborgian followers. Chapman was a member of that group, and he helped the group keep in touch with the main organization in Philadelphia. Ensign documented the fact that there were no other believers in the Swedenborgian faith living in the Mansfield area, except for Chapman, when the young minister first settled there.[5]

Chapman is mentioned in several letters written by New Church members. One, dated May 15, 1821, tells of his offer to deed one hundred sixty acres of land to the New Church in return for payment in church books. The proposal is also mentioned in a letter William Schlatter wrote to a church member in Manchester, England, on April 16, 1821: "The land that he offers is valuable and if your society had the books we would send them and receive the land and appropriate it for the use of a new Church and School and the support of a new Church minister."[6]

Historians can only guess which pieces of land Chapman considered donating to the church. In

1820, he still held ninety-nine-year leases on four quarter sections near Mansfield. Any of these could have been signed over to another party, but the new leaseholder would have had to make an interest payment immediately.

This land-for-books transfer never took place. But it is interesting to consider that Chapman was almost the founder of a religious school in the Northwest.[7]

There is little doubt that Chapman dedicated himself to missionary work. The stories were repeated time and time again. After a stop for lodging and food at some lonely settler's cabin, Chapman would pull out his Bible and offer to read some "news right fresh from Heaven."[8]

A judge, who claimed to have learned about Swedenborg from Chapman alone, said,

> His [Chapman's] main bump seemed to be to leave the books of Swedenborg whenever he could get anybody to read them, and leave them until he called again. . . . His books were very old. He got them somehow from Philadelphia. He had great thirst for making converts.[9]

## An Unusual Intellectual

Most of Chapman's acquaintances in the Ohio settlements had no idea that he was in contact with people who met in formal reading circles and academic halls. In fact, people paid little attention to the doctrine he preached. According to David

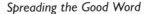

*Chapman dedicated himself to missionary work. After stopping at a settler's cabin, Chapman would pull out his Bible and offer to read some "news right fresh from Heaven."*

Ayres, whose family lived twelve miles north of Mansfield in 1815, "It was not orthodox [traditional], . . . and old Johnny was ragged."[10]

But it was not Chapman's rags that discouraged settlers from accepting his religious ideas, even though his strange looks often left people with the first impression that he was uneducated. Most settlers simply could not understand the intellectual New

Church doctrines. Chapman, however, understood them well.

Though few knew what he was talking about, Chapman did not follow his religion blindly. He read the New Church literature and discussed it intelligently. When a well-read Mansfield preacher invited Chapman to discuss religion, he was surprised to find that "the strange man of the trail had one of the best informed and most brilliant minds he had ever known."[11]

## Home Life

Several of John Chapman's family members lived in the Dexter City area, a few miles north of Marietta, Ohio. Chapman probably visited with them twice a year, since the family homestead was on his route east to collect apple seeds. After Chapman's father died in 1807, his widow, Lucy, remained in the area until her death sometime after 1810.

John's half brother Nathaniel was married and had five children. His half sister Persis married William Broom. The Brooms and their four daughters moved to Ashland County, Ohio, in 1816. Chapman hired Broom to care for his orchards. He lived with his sister and her family when he was in the area.

This appears to be the only home life that John Chapman ever knew as an adult. Though legends paint a portrait of a man who enjoyed the solitary life, other clues point to a lonely man. He was said to be very fond of his sister's children, and stayed with her family more frequently during his later years.[12] Other clues, such as his many gifts to children, his frequent visits with settlers along his route,

### A Legendary Missionary

A widespread story about Chapman is one called the "Primitive Christian." Though the setting and the minister's name seem to change with each retelling, the events are based on the original tale found in W. D. Haley's article published in *Harper's Magazine*.

Johnny Appleseed was one of a crowd that had gathered around a traveling minister. As the minister preached against sinful ways, his sermon suggested that the settlers' indulgence in such earthly pleasures of "calico cloth and store[-bought] tea" was shameful.[13] The minister continued to scold the crowd, asking: "Where now is there a man who, like the primitive Christians, is traveling to heaven barefooted and clad in coarse raiment?"

At that point, the story says, Chapman got up and went over to the speaker. Pointing to his coffee-sack clothing, Chapman said, "Here's your primitive Christian!" The traveling minister, who was quite well-dressed, suddenly seemed at a loss for words and let the group of listeners go.[14]

*This illustration of Chapman as the "Primitive Christian" was published with W. D. Haley's story "Johnny Appleseed—A Pioneer Hero."*

and his eagerness for an audience to tell stories to, indicate that Chapman longed for companionship.[15]

By 1824, fifty-year-old Chapman gave up his leased lands in north central Ohio. Once again, he focused on the idea that had first led him west. John Chapman began to expand his chain of nurseries into new frontiers.

# 8

# MONEY GROWN ON TREES

Though most people thought of John Chapman as a man living in poverty, eating only the most meager food and wearing ragged clothing, in truth, he was a good businessman—one who chose the right time to expand his business.

By the mid-1820s, many families had settled central Ohio and the market for Chapman's services moved west. The orchardist had already begun to plant seeds along rivers in the northwest corner of the state where much of the land was made up of bogs, swamps, and marshes. Until this time, these wetlands had discouraged homesteaders.

## Dedicated Businessman

There is evidence that Chapman was making his rounds in the area by at least 1828. One early settler remembered the trees his parents selected from a boatload of seedlings that year. The young trees came from Chapman's nursery near present-day Findlay, Ohio.

The pioneer remembered the date clearly because a year later, his family found safety among those transplanted saplings. After a very heavy rain, the mother and two children were driven from their cabin by a flood. They waded through water for a quarter of a mile before reaching high ground, just "where the first orchard was planted in the [previous] year, the trees being purchased of John Chapman. . . ."[1]

Chapman soon extended his nurseries into northeastern Indiana. Several different dates have been given for his first trip to Fort Wayne. Stories handed down by pioneer families have him arriving there when the frontier town was still little more than a trading post built near Mad Anthony Wayne's fort.

Although there is no solid proof of Chapman's presence until 1836, an article printed in the *Fort Wayne Sentinel* in October 1871 supports an earlier date. One settler, who knew Chapman and saw him many times, told this story:

*Chapman would throw a bag of apple seeds over his shoulder, walk to a fertile spot, and plant his seeds. Then he would move on, leaving his seeds to sprout and grow.*

> John Chapman came here long before [1836]. . . .
> Certain it is, that in 1830 he was seen one autumn
> day, seated in a section of hollow tree he had
> improvised for a boat, and filled with apple seeds
> fresh from the cider presses of a more eastern part of
> the country, paddling up the Maumee River—and
> landing at Wayne's fort, at the foot of main street,
> Fort Wayne. He kept the seed wet for preservation;
> his boat was daubed with mud and tree moss. . . .[2]

Dugouts—boats made from hollowed out logs—
were common transportation at that time. Chapman
often used these crude canoes to carry his seeds. He
probably followed the easiest course to reach Fort
Wayne, floating down the St. Mary River with the
current. He is said to have planted his first nursery
in 1828 along the St. Joseph River, a stream that
meets the St. Mary River to form the Maumee River
near the fort. After sowing his seeds, Chapman most
likely returned to central Ohio, by way of another
downstream ride on the Maumee River, to Defiance,
then from there up the Auglaise and Blanchard
rivers to Mansfield.

## Orchards to Tend

More clearly than ever before, the seasons now reg-
ulated John Chapman's routine. Each spring, he
would follow the rivers through northeastern Ohio
into Indiana, stopping to tend his young trees or sell
the seedlings to pioneers. Then, as apple harvest
time approached in the fall, Chapman would return
to his winter home near Mansfield. Year after year,

## Legendary Travels

Legends suggest that John Chapman traveled across the Midwest and met other well-known historical figures, such as Daniel Boone in Kentucky and Abraham Lincoln in Illinois. Trees the orchardist planted are said to have taken root in southern Michigan. He supposedly even sang folk songs in northern Missouri. A Knox County historian suggested that Chapman may have traveled as far as Iowa. The information came from a county resident who recalled "that in the fall of 1843 . . . Johnny Appleseed passed through the country [Illinois] on foot, and stopped all night . . . stating that he was then from the Iowa prairies on his way to a Swedenborgian Convention in Philadelphia."[3]

However, no proof exists that the real John Chapman ever traveled more than a few miles west of Fort Wayne. As in Ohio, many places in Indiana and across the Midwest claim to have Johnny Appleseed trees and traditions. None of these can be overlooked—but few can be verified.

records show his regular trail and the time devoted to his trees.

For his largest nurseries, Chapman often constructed a crude shelter nearby or arranged to board with a local farmer. For example, in 1836, Chapman bought land in Jay County, Indiana, about forty-five

miles south of Fort Wayne. He planted seeds the next year and boarded with a farmer in the neighborhood for twelve weeks. In 1838, Chapman spent eighteen weeks with the same family while he tended his seedlings. In 1839, his boarding bill was for ten weeks.

After that, it seemed that much shorter periods were needed to care for and maintain a nursery. Chapman boarded with the Jay County family for only two, three, or four weeks each year after 1840. Most likely, this pattern was repeated again and again as the nurseryman tended his chain of orchards.

John Chapman was responsible for extensive plantings of apple trees throughout the Midwest. However, he could not claim that his seedlings always produced the best fruit. Chapman always grew his trees from seed. Even if the seed came from a high quality apple, the new trees often produced fruit that was small, mealy, and tasteless. Today, no nurseryman would plant orchards from the seed of his favorite apple and expect the trees to produce the same delicious fruit. We know that the only reliable way to produce trees with identical fruit is to graft, or implant, a bud onto the stem of a seedling.

Better trees were available even in Chapman's time. Orchardists along the east coast grafted apple trees to improve the quality of fruit. They inserted

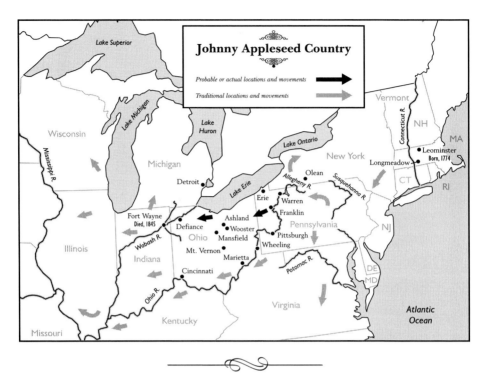

*John Chapman planted trees in a wide area through what are now the states of Ohio and Indiana.*

buds from a tree that produced desirable apples onto the trunks and branches of new seedlings. However, transportation of grafted stock into the Midwest was expensive. Few settlers could have afforded the trees.

Whatever the quality of the fruit that grew on Chapman's trees, pioneers found a use for it. If it was not good enough to eat right off the tree, they made apple butter, cider, or sliced the fruit and dried it.

**Dried Apples**

In the fall, pioneers dried large quantities of apples. After the apples were peeled, cored, and quartered, they were spread out on drying platforms. Soon, the apples would be covered with bees, wasps, and sucking flies. These insects sucked the moisture from the slices and helped the apples dry more quickly. The slices were turned several times until they were perfectly dry, ready to string on cord and hang from the rafters, until needed to make sauces during the winter months when fresh fruit was unavailable.

Actually, a few of Chapman's seedlings produced fairly good fruit. Occasionally, some would even produce superior apples. Once the young trees grew bigger, a farmer could improve his orchard by grafting buds from his best trees onto others that were not as good.

## Canals Open New Territory

In the 1800s, settlers moving west traveled mostly by rivers. These waterways provided the easiest travel routes. Most early settlers to the Indiana Territory stayed near the Ohio River. That changed around 1826, when the United States government decided to build the Wabash and Erie Canal. The canal was to link the Maumee River, which emptied

**A Rose by Any Other Name . . .**
The apple tree, a deciduous plant that loses its leaves each year, is related to the rose family. The native home of the fruit is not known for certain, but the tree probably originated in the area between the Caspian and the Black seas in Europe. Remnants of apples have been found in prehistoric lake dwellings in Switzerland. Apples were also a favorite fruit of the ancient Romans. When they conquered England, it is believed they took the fruit with them.

Early settlers brought apple seeds and trees to America from England. Records of the Massachusetts Bay Company indicate that John Endicott, one of the colony's first governors, planted trees in New England as early as 1630. Seeds were carried west by traders, American Indians, and of course, John Chapman.

into Lake Erie at Toledo, Ohio, to the Wabash River near present-day Huntington, Indiana.

The first section of canal, between Fort Wayne and Huntington, was begun in 1832 and completed in 1835. However, builders soon realized that most boats could not navigate that far up the Wabash. The water level was sometimes not deep enough, so the canal was extended west to the Tippecanoe River just above Lafayette, Indiana.

The Maumee River also did not provide a reliable water route, so the canal was extended again, east of Fort Wayne. Eventually, the Wabash and Erie

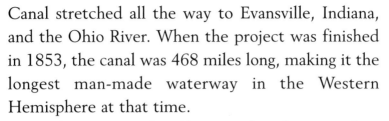

Canal stretched all the way to Evansville, Indiana, and the Ohio River. When the project was finished in 1853, the canal was 468 miles long, making it the longest man-made waterway in the Western Hemisphere at that time.

In the 1830s, John Chapman bought more than forty-two acres along the Maumee River about three miles outside of Fort Wayne. The land sold for $2.50 per acre, and Chapman paid cash. He also purchased ninety-nine acres priced at $1.50 per acre, three miles farther north, almost on the Ohio border.

Chapman planted nurseries near the canal route. He was ready and waiting when the canals began to carry a steady flow of new settlers to northeastern Indiana. In fact, by 1838, one of his largest nurseries in the Fort Wayne area boasted fifteen thousand trees—trees he had planted at least six to eight years before.

At the age of sixty-two, Chapman was still buying real estate in Indiana. On March 10, 1836, he paid cash for nineteen more acres near one of his first parcels. One day later, he bought seventy-four acres along the Wabash River in Jay County, near present-day New Corydon, Indiana. Two years later, the orchardist bought forty acres northwest of Fort Wayne. By 1838, Indiana had become Chapman's home base and the trees from his nurseries were bearing fruit in a dozen Indiana counties.

*Canal boats like this one brought people and produce to the Fort Wayne area, where Chapman had apple trees ready to sell.*

## His Own Ways

Not many people knew much about the orchardist's business. Chapman himself seems to have been the only one who knew all the property he owned. Perhaps he deliberately allowed people to believe he was just a poor old man who wandered the frontier, planting apple seeds. Contrary to popular belief, Chapman sometimes carried large amounts of money as he traveled between Indiana and Ohio.

One story handed down by family members tells of a time when Chapman feared that thieves would rob him. He crawled into a cave-like hole under a large tree, hid his money under the roots, and left it there for three years. Another time, Chapman is said to have climbed to the roof of his cabin and stuck his money under the clapboards, or rough wooden shingles.[4] Such hiding places were common among wilderness settlers.

It does appear that businessmen in the Fort Wayne area knew Chapman had money and extended him credit. Records show he used that credit to buy a pocketknife costing seventy-five cents on February 22, 1840. The Hamilton-Taber & Company ledger carried the account under the name of John Appleseed. The account was settled on April 8, 1840, when Chapman paid cash for the knife. Compared to the cost of land ($1.50 to $2.50 per acre), the pocket knife seemed very expensive.

During the last years of his life, Chapman owned parcels of land that totaled more than three hundred fifty acres in Ohio and Indiana—land bought with the cash Chapman earned with his chain of nurseries. While this did not make Chapman a wealthy man, he did own more than the average settler in the Midwest.

# 9

# FINAL SEASONS

During the last five years of his life, Chapman devoted most of his time to his Indiana orchards. Records show that he owned five large parcels, but he seemed to have developed only two into nurseries. A forty-two-acre tract along the Maumee River was one of Chapman's largest orchards. It had fifteen thousand seedlings growing in it.

The only other plot Chapman improved was in Jay County, about forty miles south of Fort Wayne. With the help of his brother-in-law William Broom, the orchardist built a log cabin and cut timbers to build a barn. William Broom, his wife, Persis, and their children had followed Chapman west and settled near his property. It is believed that Chapman was planning to make his home in Jay County.[1]

## The Country Continues to Grow

By the 1840s, the United States was growing in size. In addition to the vast lands acquired in the 1803 Louisiana Purchase, the United States, in 1845, would make Texas a state. By this time, the frontier had moved west of Johnny Appleseed country to the foothills of the Rocky Mountains.

Chapman would have noticed many changes as he continued to make regular visits to his family in Ohio. By this time, cities and towns had sprung up all over the state. Most of the land was now settled. Roads crisscrossed the land, and by the time of his last visit, there were canals and even railroads. Simple log cabins were abandoned. Homes were now built of brick or milled lumber.

In October 1842, sixty-eight-year-old Chapman made his last known visit to his brother Nathaniel's family in southern Ohio. A neighbor recalled this trip and a special gift the orchardist received:

> While on his last visit, his niece, Miss Rebecka Chapman (a daughter of Nathaniel's) made him a shirt, one half of calico, the other muslin. On the one [made] of the muslin, were two large letters, perhaps A. D. These he had so arranged that one was on either side of the bosom. That seemed to please him.[2]

No one knows what the letters stood for.

Chapman made his last trip to the home of his favorite niece shortly before his death. Lucy Jane Broom, a daughter of Persis and William, had married William Johns. The couple settled east of the Fort Wayne area near Van Wert, Ohio.

## Time to Rest

An obituary published in the March 22, 1845, edition of the *Fort Wayne Sentinel* provides all the factual details of John Chapman's death that were recorded at that time. The notice read:

> The deceased was well known through this region by his eccentricity, and the strange garb he usually wore. He followed the occupation of a nurseryman, and has been a regular visitor here upwards of 20 years. He was a native of Pennsylvania but his home—if home he had—for some years past was in the neighborhood of Cleveland, O[hio], where he has relatives living. He is supposed to have considerable property, yet he denied himself almost the common necessities of life—not so much perhaps from avarice [greed] as from his peculiar notions on religious subjects. . . .
>
> In the most inclement weather he might be seen barefooted and almost naked except when he chanced to pick up articles of old clothing. Notwithstanding the privations and exposure he endured he lived to an extremely old age, not less than 80 years at the time of his death—though no person would have judged from his appearance that he was 60 [he was actually seventy]. He always carried with him some work on the doctrine of Swedenborg, with which he was perfectly familiar, and would readily converse and argue. . . . His death was quite sudden. He was seen on our streets a day or two previous.[3]

While the published obituary does establish the date of John Chapman's death with reasonable certainty, no one agrees about the circumstances. According to the most common story, Chapman was working at one of his nurseries when he received a message that cattle had broken into another one, twenty miles away near Fort Wayne.

The orchardist left right away on foot. When he reached Fort Wayne after only one day of travel, Chapman arranged to stay with a Mr. Worth. Unfortunately, the hard journey was too much for

*This glass flask is a gift that Chapman is said to have given to a little girl who lived in Fort Wayne.*

**A Legendary Death**

Because Chapman's obituary left much to the imagination, storytellers have created many romantic and sentimental tales of Johnny Appleseed's death and burial. One version included his last supper with the Worths and the reading of his favorite passage from the Bible: "Blessed are the pure of heart."[4] Then the old gentleman went to his eternal rest, at peace with the world. Neighbors supposedly came from miles around to hear the funeral sermon. The pallbearers were the most prominent men in Fort Wayne and, again, apple blossoms drifted silently down upon the coffin—a beautiful, fitting ending for the legend.

the seventy-year-old man. He is said to have died during the night or after a short illness.

Winter plague, probably a form of pneumonia, is generally accepted as the cause of Chapman's death. Most agree that he died at the Worth home, located on the west bank of the St. Joseph River near one of Chapman's nurseries. Mr. Worth's first name could not be determined—David, Richard, and William Worth all lived along the St. Joseph River at that time.

Samuel C. Fetter, the man who prepared Chapman's body for burial and made his black walnut coffin, provided this report of the old gentleman's attire when he died:

His shirt was a coarse coffee sack—a hole cut in the center for his head. He had the waists of four pairs of pants cut off at the forks [the crotch], ripped up the sides; the fronts thrown away and the hinder parts were buttoned around him—lapping like shingles to cover the lower parts of his body; and all over these a pair of what had once been pantaloons.[5]

And so, John Chapman was buried in a pioneer family cemetery on a shady knoll overlooking the St. Joseph River near Fort Wayne, Indiana. His final resting place was only about ten miles from the location of one of his largest nurseries.

## A Fruitful Inheritance?

Soon after Chapman died, John Harold, the husband of one of Persis Broom's daughters, traveled to Fort Wayne from Jay County to gather information about Chapman's estate. After a week's investigation, Harold asked the Allen County Circuit Court to give him the authority to settle his uncle's affairs.

The inventory of items Harold listed as part of Chapman's estate included: a gray mare, thousands of seedlings, and five parcels of land in Allen and Jay counties—assets totaling about six hundred dollars.

Harold then worked several more months collecting claims against Chapman's estate from family members and others who had extended credit to the orchardist: a bill from William Broom for improvements appraised at $155; a second bill from Broom for $127.68; a boarding bill from a Jay County

*In 1916, the Indiana Horticultural Society selected a spot to memorialize Chapman. In 1935, the Optimist Club of Fort Wayne erected a natural granite boulder brought from the nursery site on the Maumee where Chapman had fifteen thousand seedlings growing when he died. The inscription reads: "He lived for others."*

farmer for $8.75; Worth's bill for $19.44 to cover Chapman's funeral; and Harold's own expenses of $67.62.[6]

Chapman's nephew by marriage kept the gray mare valued at seventeen dollars and five hundred apples trees worth fifteen dollars. These items seem to be all he received for his time.

At that point, the estate, including fifteen hundred apple trees, was turned over to a lawyer. Eventually, he sold much of the property, but Chapman's half sister (probably Persis), received only $165.95. The lawyer claimed most of the income as his fee for settling the estate.

In addition, six hundred dollars' worth of claims against the estate were never paid. Among the outstanding debts were two mementos of the orchardist's earlier years: IOUs signed by Chapman in February 1804 to Nathaniel Chapman for "one hundred dollars in land or apple trees with interest till paid;" and to the children of Nathaniel and Elizabeth Rudd for "one hundred dollars to be paid and interest till they become of age."[7] It is not known who presented these claims to his estate.

# THE LEGEND GROWS

Today, people love to hear stories of the kindly hermit, Johnny Appleseed, who planted trees across the frontier ahead of the pioneers. He is often mentioned as part of America's frontier folklore, along with lumberjack Paul Bunyan and John Henry, the steel-driving railroad man. But unlike these last two figures, Johnny Appleseed was a real person—John Chapman.

The seeds of his legend were planted long before Chapman's death in 1845. Storytellers, especially those living in central Ohio, did their best to nurture these tales. However, it was not until an article by W. D. Haley appeared in the November 1871 issue of *Harper's New Monthly Magazine*, that the legend burst into full bloom.

Haley's piece, entitled "Johnny Appleseed—A Pioneer Hero," spread the story across the country. Bits of Haley's account can be found in almost all stories written about the legendary frontiersman after that time. In the introduction of his article, Haley wrote: "Among the heroes of endurance that was voluntary, and of action that was creative . . . , there was one man whose name, seldom mentioned now save by some of the few surviving pioneers, deserves to be perpetuated."[1]

Haley, who lived in central Ohio, gathered material for the article, "chiefly from memories of old residents who remembered Johnny."[2] However, he definitely exaggerated many aspects of Johnny Appleseed's character and life history. Much of Haley's information came from Rosella Rice, a local novel writer. Rice was born about the time Chapman left central Ohio for northern Indiana. Most likely, she only saw the orchardist during his annual trips back to central Ohio.

The most lasting portrait of John Chapman developed during his last years in Indiana. That image of a saintly, white-haired, ragged old man became so popular that he is usually portrayed that way—even in stories of his early years.

Hundreds of so-called reminiscences and family stories about Chapman were recorded by pioneers

who lived in the Fort Wayne area. Many were obviously inspired by the *Harper's* article that made Johnny Appleseed a legendary hero. However, one historian in Jay County had recorded these recollections before that, in 1864:

> Among the pioneers of Jay was an oddity called Johnny Appleseed. . . . Many years ago he brought from Central Ohio, two bushels of apple-seed, on the back of an ox, and cleared small patches of ground . . . and planted apple-seeds.
>
> In the early settlement of this county, he was wandering about from one nursery to another, camping wherever night overtook him, selling trees. . . . He never carried a gun or wore a sound piece of clothing, though he possessed considerable property; never slept in a bed, or ate at a table; had no place he called home; was a devoted Swedenborgian in religion, and died near Fort Wayne in 1845.[3]

The many stories about Johnny Appleseed take him to widely spread places for an extraordinary number of adventures. With the things we know the real man accomplished, he would hardly have had the time to do all these things. However, it is not surprising that these stories grew, since many pioneer families only saw Chapman at a certain time of year. No doubt they wondered what he did with the rest of his time. They did not know he was tending his chain of orchards—and inspiring legends—in other territories.

Chapman's legend grew because he left no written record. We will never be absolutely sure which

**Uncovering the Facts**

The facts of John Chapman's life might forever have been disguised by legend if not for the investigation of another man. Dr. Robert Price spent almost twenty-five years carefully researching and writing his well-documented biography of John Chapman, *Johnny Appleseed, Man and Myth*, which was published in 1954.

Price began with pioneer family stories handed down from one generation to another. He relied on the work of Fort Wayne educator Robert C. Harris, who carefully collected and preserved the few solid records that document John Chapman's life. Price also used the genealogical research of Florence Wheeler, a librarian in Leominster, Massachusetts. Wheeler worked for years and finally traced the ancestors of John Chapman.

tales are based on fact and which are pure fiction. But maybe that is not really necessary. As one writer observed, "the truth is, of course, that Johnny Appleseed has attained that legendary status where the facts are no longer important."[4]

And it has been with these legends that storytellers have impressed generations of children—tales that have been embellished until it appears that John Chapman planted nearly every apple orchard in the Midwest and across the country. Connecticut, Massachusetts, Vermont, Tennessee, Missouri, Iowa, Nebraska, Wisconsin, the Rocky Mountain states, and

*Many towns across the Midwest hold Johnny Appleseed festivals each year in September.*

even the Pacific Coast region all claim to have trees planted by Johnny Appleseed.

## The Seeds Planted

John Chapman deserves credit for planting many apple orchards in Ohio and Indiana—not a small feat for one man to accomplish. And while we do not want to overlook the orchardist's important work of bringing fruit into the wilderness, Chapman's legacy stretches far beyond the apples from his trees, to the seeds he planted in storytellers' imaginations. His greatest and most abundant gifts have been handed down as folktales.

American writers quickly discovered the story of John Chapman. They recognized the picturesque quality of his frontier setting. They grasped the meaningful message in the life of the unselfish, useful pioneer planter. Even before the *Harper's* article appeared in 1871, several poets and novelists, including Rosella Rice, had written poems and stories about Johnny Appleseed.

Today, researchers can list hundreds of titles in a bibliography about Johnny Appleseed. The Allen County Public Library in Fort Wayne has more than seventy-five listed in its catalog system, and that does not include all the articles and clippings preserved in a file folder.

The spirit of John Chapman has been preserved in picture books, plays, novels, and biographies. He

has been depicted on audio tape, filmstrips, and in animated films complete with musical scores.

The story of his life is still popular today. With every anniversary of his birth and death, articles are published about his marathon run during the War of 1812, about places he once slept, and even about

**Apple-Seed John**

This poem by Lydia Maria Child, an American writer who started the first monthly magazine for children in the United States in 1826, is one of the oldest written about the orchardist. It was first published in 1880:

> Poor Johnny was bended well-nigh double
> With years of toil, and care, and trouble;
> But his large old heart still felt the need
> Of doing for others some kindly deed . . .
> Old Johnny said: . . . "There's a way for me!"
> He worked, and he worked with might and main,
> But no one knew the plan in his brain.
> He took ripe apples in pay for chores,
> And carefully cut from them all the cores.
> He filled a bag full then wandered away,
> And no man saw him for many a day. . . .
> With pointed cane deep holes he would bore,
> And in every hole he placed a core;
> Then covered them well, and left them there
> In keeping of sunshine, rain and air. . . .
> And so, as time passed and traveled on,
> Everyone called him "Old Apple-Seed John."[5]

trees the legendary man supposedly planted that still bear fruit.

## Remembered for All Time

Though John Chapman is gone, and most of the trees he planted no longer bear fruit, he has not been forgotten in the Midwest or, for that matter, across the country. A monument has been placed near the site of his birth. The simple granite marker is located on Johnny Appleseed Lane, in Leominster, Massachusetts.

The old Mansfield blockhouse has been preserved in a city park, along with a sign describing the legend of Chapman's midnight run. Near Dexter City, Ohio, a monument in his honor stands along a highway at the foot of a hill below an old cemetery where Chapman's half brother and other members of his family are buried.

The Johnny Appleseed Memorial Park in Fort Wayne includes the traditional site of Chapman's grave. Viewed by many visitors annually, the grave is marked by a boulder and surrounded by an iron fence.

In 1966, the United States Postal Service remembered Johnny Appleseed with a commemorative five-cent stamp. Even today, trees are planted in his honor. Schools, parks, and bridges are named after him. Many towns across the Midwest hold Johnny Appleseed festivals in September.

NEAR THIS SITE WAS BORN
JOHN CHAPMAN
KNOWN AS
JOHNNY APPLESEED
SEPT. 26, 1774        MAR. 18, 1845
LEOMINSTER HISTORICAL SOCIETY
1963

*Chapman's birthplace has been commemorated in Leominster, Massachusetts, with this marker. It sits on a quiet residential street near the edge of the small community.*

### A Legendary Ghost

According to an article in the *Columbus Citizen* on September 26, 1943, Johnny Appleseed's ghost returns every year to the family cemetery on the hill near Dexter City, Ohio, where Chapman's father and family once lived. The report said:

> a small boy on his way one morning to gather nuts was astonished to see a gray-bearded twinkling-eyed old man, barefooted, mushpot on head, poised on an apple bough up in the cemetery. The stranger was munching an apple and reading a tract of Swedenborg. Shortly afterward, a mailman going to deliver to a mother a letter from her soldier son overseas was surprised by the same apparition [ghost]. And a little while later a woman on her way to help a sick neighbor also saw it.[6]

Not everyone can see the ghost, however, storytellers add—only the good and innocent.

Near Mansfield, Ohio, is the Johnny Appleseed Heritage Center. It includes an interactive museum with exhibits about Chapman's life and the region. It also has an outdoor amphitheater, the setting for a two-hour musical drama that celebrates the man with the best qualities of pioneers—independence, resourcefulness, and courage—adding one more tale to help keep John Chapman's story and spirit alive for generations to come.

# CHRONOLOGY

1769— Nathaniel Chapman and Elizabeth Simons married in Leominster, Massachusetts, in August.

1774— John Chapman born in Leominster, Massachusetts, on September 26.

1776— Nathaniel Chapman born, June 26; John's mother, Elizabeth, died, July 18; Nathaniel died within two weeks of Elizabeth's death.

1780— Nathaniel Chapman married Lucy Cooley, in July; Nathaniel Chapman dismissed from the army, September 30; Elizabeth and John probably went to live with father and stepmother in Longmeadow, Massachusetts.

1797— John Chapman probably began travels west, reaching Pennsylvania near town of Warren.

1801— Possible record of name by the federal census in Franklin, Pennsylvania; Entered the Ohio Territory for the first time.

1804— Signed two IOUs in Franklin.

1805— Nathaniel Chapman, John's father, settled near Marietta, Ohio, with wife and children.

1806— John Chapman sold apple trees in Mount Vernon, Ohio.

1807— Nathaniel Chapman, John's father, died and was buried near Marietta, Ohio.

1809— John Chapman bought two town lots in Mount Vernon, Ohio, for orchards.

1812— Made legendary run to warn settlers living near Mansfield, Ohio, of possible Indian attack in September.

1815— Purchased or leased large sections of land in central Ohio for orchards.

**1816**— Presented a Fourth of July address in Huron County, Ohio.

**1817**— Report of his missionary service for Swedenborgian Church appears in Manchester Society Bulletin.

**1821**— Offered to deed land to Swedenborgian Church in return for books published by the church.

**1828**— Planted orchards in northeastern Ohio.

**1830**— Extended his orchards to Fort Wayne, Indiana, area; Bought land and planted first orchard along the St. Joseph River.

**1836**— Bought land in Jay County, Indiana.

**1842**— Last known visit with half brother Nathaniel near Marietta, Ohio.

**1845**— Died at age seventy, near Fort Wayne, Indiana, on March 18.

# CHAPTER NOTES

**Chapter 1. The Midnight Run of John Chapman**

1. Robert Price, *Johnny Appleseed, Man and Myth* (Bloomington: Indiana University Press, 1954), p. 88.

2. Ibid., pp. 88–89.

3. A. J. Baughman, "Historical Sketch of the Life and Work of 'Johnny Appleseed,'" Proceedings of Richland Co. Historical Society, Salem, n.d., p. 26.

4. W. D. Haley, "Johnny Appleseed—A Pioneer Hero," *Harper's New Monthly Magazine*, vol. XLIII, November 1871, p. 833.

5. Price, p. 95.

6. Harlan Hatcher, Robert Price, Florence Murdoch, John W. Stockwell, Ophia D. Smith, Leslie Marshall, *Johnny Appleseed, A Voice in the Wilderness, The Story of the Pioneer John Chapman* (Paterson, N.J.: The Swedenborg Press, 1945), p. 33.

**Chapter 2. The Minuteman's Son**

1. Robert Price, *Johnny Appleseed, Man and Myth* (Bloomington: Indiana University Press, 1954), p. 279.

2. Julie Lawlor, *The Real Johnny Appleseed* (Morton Grove, Ill.: Albert Whitman & Company, 1995), pp. 11–12.

3. Mabel Leigh Hunt, *Better Known as Johnny Appleseed* (New York: J. B. Lippincott Company, 1950), p. 9.

4. Ibid., p. 10.

5. Lawlor, p. 18.

6. Price, p. 12.

7. Hunt, p. 5.

8. Lawlor, p. 14.

9. "Facts About Chapmans in Leominster," Leominster Public Library, n.d., p. 1.

10. Robert C. Harris, *Johnny Appleseed Sourcebook* (Fort Wayne, Ind.: Public Library of Fort Wayne and Allen County, 1949), pp. 1–2.

11. Price, p. 280.

## Chapter 3. Growing up With a New Country

1. Steven Fortriede, *Johnny Appleseed: The Man Behind the Myth* (Fort Wayne, Ind.: Public Library of Fort Wayne and Allen County, 1978), p. 1.

2. Robert Price, *Johnny Appleseed, Man and Myth* (Bloomington: Indiana University Press, 1954), p. 17.

3. Fortriede, pp. 2–3.

4. Harlan Hatcher, Robert Price, Florence Murdoch, John W. Stockwell, Ophia D. Smith, Leslie Marshall, *Johnny Appleseed, A Voice in the Wilderness, The Story of the Pioneer John Chapman* (Paterson, N.J.: The Swedenborg Press, 1945), p. 48.

5. H. Kenneth Dirlam, *John Chapman—By Occupation a Gatherer and Planter of Apple Seeds* (Mansfield, Ohio: Richland County Ohio Sesquicentennial Committee, 1953), p. 5.

## Chapter 4. Blown in by a Blizzard

1. Steven Fortriede, *Johnny Appleseed: The Man Behind the Myth* (Fort Wayne, Ind.: Public Library of Fort Wayne and Allen County, 1978), p. 6.

2. Robert Price, *Johnny Appleseed, Man and Myth* (Bloomington: Indiana University Press, 1954), p. 8.

3. Ibid., p. 33.

4. Fortriede, p. 3.

5. Ibid., pp. 5–6.

6. Price, p. 28.

7. Richard Battin, "'Mad Anthony' Wayne at Fallen Timbers," *Fort Wayne, Indiana, News-Sentinel*, n.d., <http://earlyamerica.com/review/fall96/anthony.html> (April 1999).

8. Ibid.

9. "The Treaty of Greenville," *The University of Oklahoma Law Center*, August 3, 1795, <http://www.law.ou.edu/greenvil.html> (April 1999).

10. Fortriede, p. 5.

## Chapter 5. Across the Northwest Territory

1. H. Kenneth Dirlam, "Johnny Appleseed," Richland County Historical Society, Mansfield, Ohio, n.d., p. 8.

2. Gary S. Williams, *Johnny Appleseed in the Duck Creek Valley* (Dexter City, Ohio: Johnny Appleseed Center for Creative Learning, 1989), p. 2.

3. W. D. Haley, "Johnny Appleseed—A Pioneer Hero," *Harper's New Monthly Magazine*, vol. XLIII, November 1871, p. 831.

4. Ibid., p. 832.

5. Harlan Hatcher, Robert Price, Florence Murdoch, John W. Stockwell, Ophia D. Smith, Leslie Marshall, *Johnny Appleseed, A Voice in the Wilderness, The Story of the Pioneer John Chapman* (Paterson, N.J.: The Swedenborg Press, 1945), p. 61.

6. Haley, p. 830.

7. Steven Fortriede, *Johnny Appleseed: The Man Behind the Myth* (Fort Wayne, Ind.: Public Library of Fort Wayne and Allen County, 1978), p. 7.

8. Haley, p. 831.

9. Fortriede, p. 10.

10. Hatcher et al., p. 62.

11. Olive Beaupre Miller, *Old Johnny Appleseed* (Fort Wayne, Ind.: Staff of the Public Library of Fort Wayne and Allen County, 1955), p. 8.

12. Haley, p. 835.

13. Ibid.

14. Williams, p. 14.

## Chapter 6. The War of 1812

1. Harlan Hatcher, Robert Price, Florence Murdoch, John W. Stockwell, Ophia D. Smith, Leslie Marshall, *Johnny Appleseed, A Voice in the Wilderness, The Story of the Pioneer John Chapman* (Paterson, N.J.: The Swedenborg Press, 1945), p. 55.

2. Ibid.

3. W. D. Haley, "Johnny Appleseed—A Pioneer Hero," *Harper's New Monthly Magazine*, vol. XLIII, November 1871, p. 832.

4. Hatcher et al., pp. 55–56.

5. Robert Price, *Johnny Appleseed, Man and Myth* (Bloomington: Indiana University Press, 1954), pp. 83–84.

6. Ibid., p. 99.

7. James Lattimore Himrod, *The True Story of Jonathan Chapman, by the Grandson of One Who Knew Him Well* (Chicago: Ten Brook-Viquesney, Co., 1926), pp. 16–17.

8. Hatcher et al., p. 61.

9. Ibid., p. 60.

## Chapter 7. Spreading the Good Word

1. Robert C. Harris, *Johnny Appleseed Sourcebook* (Fort Wayne, Ind.: Public Library of Fort Wayne and Allen County, 1949), p. 8.

2. "Emmanuel Swedenborg", n.d., <http://www.swedenborg.org/swedenb.html> (April 1999).

3. Harris, p. 9.

4. Ibid., p. 11.

5. Robert Price, *Johnny Appleseed, Man and Myth* (Bloomington: Indiana University Press, 1954), p. 126.

6. Harris, p. 9.

7. Price, p. 130.

8. Steven Fortriede, *Johnny Appleseed: The Man Behind the Myth* (Fort Wayne, Ind.: Fort Wayne Public Library, 1978), p. 15.

9. Price, p. 133.

10. Ibid., p. 135.

11. Ibid., p. 134.

12. Virgil A. Stanfield, "Appleseed Planted Tree and a Legend," *The News Journal*, September 19, 1982, p. 1.

13. W. D. Haley, "Johnny Appleseed—A Pioneer Hero," *Harper's New Monthly Magazine*, vol. XLIII, November 1871, p. 835.

14. Ibid.

15. Price, p. 148.

## Chapter 8. Money Grown on Trees

1. Robert Price, *Johnny Appleseed, Man and Myth* (Bloomington: Indiana University Press, 1954), pp. 190–191.

2. H. Kenneth Dirlam, "Johnny Appleseed," Richland County Historical Society, Mansfield, Ohio, n.d., p. 2.

3. Price, p. 218.

4. Ibid., p. 152.

## Chapter 9. Final Seasons

1. H. Kenneth Dirlam, *Johnny Appleseed* (Mansfield, Ohio: Richland County Historical Society), p. 9.

2. Gary S. Williams, *Johnny Appleseed in the Duck Creek Valley* (Dexter City, Ohio: Johnny Appleseed Center for Creative Learning, 1989), p. 23.

3. "Obituary Notice," *Indiana Historical Bulletin*, vol. 11, 1933–1934, no. 12, p. 393.

4. Steven Fortriede, *Johnny Appleseed: The Man Behind the Myth* (Fort Wayne, Ind.: Public Library of Fort Wayne and Allen County, 1978), p. 29.

5. Dirlam, p. 9.

6. Robert C. Harris, *Johnny Appleseed Sourcebook* (Fort Wayne, Ind.: Public Library of Fort Wayne and Allen County, 1949), pp. 22–23.

7. Ibid., p. 3.

## Chapter 10. The Legend Grows

1. W. D. Haley, "Johnny Appleseed—A Pioneer Hero," *Harper's New Monthly Magazine*, vol. XLIII, November 1871, p. 830.

2. Harlan Hatcher, Robert Price, Florence Murdoch, John W. Stockwell, Ophia D. Smith, Leslie Marshall, *Johnny Appleseed, A Voice in the Wilderness, The Story of the Pioneer John Chapman* (Paterson, N.J.: The Swedenborg Press, 1945), p. 10.

3. Robert Price, *Johnny Appleseed, Man and Myth* (Bloomington: Indiana University Press, 1954), pp. 209–210.

4. Gary S. Williams, *Johnny Appleseed in the Duck Creek Valley* (Dexter City, Ohio: Johnny Appleseed Center for Creative Learning, 1989), p. 3.

5. Hatcher et al., p. 23.

6. Williams, p. 20.

# GLOSSARY

**blockhouse**—Log fort built to provide a safe refuge for frontier settlers during an attack.

**Continental Congress**—Assembly of representatives of the American colonies during the Revolutionary period.

**doctrines**—Religious teachings.

**flint and steel**—Fire-starting tools carried by frontiersmen.

**garrison**—Troops stationed in a fort.

**Great Spirit**—An American Indian name for God.

**heathen**—A person who is not a religious believer.

**legend**—Story handed down for generations that is believed to have a historical basis.

**magistrates**—Minor officials who are empowered to enforce the law.

**muster**—To assemble troops.

**New Church**—Another name for the Swedenborgian Church.

**orchardist**—Person who cultivates orchards.

**resolution**—Formal statement.

**Swedenborgian**—Having to do with the church founded upon the writings of Emanuel Swedenborg.

**War Hawks**—Members of the United States Congress in the 1800s who strongly urged the United States to declare war against Great Britain.

# FURTHER READING

Berton, Pierre. *The Death of Tecumseh*. Toronto, Ontario, Canada: McClelland & Stewart, 1998.

Franch, Irene M., and David M. Brownstone. *The American Way West*. New York: Facts on File, 1991.

Hakim, Joy. *From Colonies to Country*. New York: Oxford University Press, 1993.

Isham, Bruce. *Johnny Appleseed*. Margate, Tasmania: Bandicoot Books, 1998.

Kellogg, Steven. *Johnny Appleseed: A Tall Tale Retold*. New York: Morrow, 1988.

Lawlor, Laurie, *The Real Johnny Appleseed*. Morton Grove, Ill.: Albert Whitman & Company, 1995.

Marrin, Albert. *Eighteen Twelve: The War Nobody Won*. New York: Atheneum, 1985.

# INTERNET ADDRESSES

*The Johnny Appleseed Festival*. December 7, 1999. <http://johnnyappleseedfest.com/> (July 13, 2000).

*The Johnny Appleseed Homepage*. April 11, 1996. <http://www.msc.cornell.edu/~weeds/SchoolPages/Appleseed/welcome.html/> (July 13, 2000).

# INDEX